NOTES ON THIS SERIES OF SIGNALLING DIAGRA

GENERAL

It is intended that this volume will be one of a series that will eventually cover much of the west country and Southern England, and will make public the author's vast collection of data.
The published information represents many years of research, but even so, some signal boxes - notably those closed in the 1930's, seem to have vanished without leaving any official records.
The collection cannot therefore claim to be complete, although in some areas total coverage has been possible.
The amount of information also varies widely from place to place, and the listed alterations do not represent a full history of the signal boxes in most cases.
For small layouts where the alterations have been few, one diagram with suitable notes is usually sufficient, but at locations that have undergone considerable remodelling several drawings are necessary.

The diagrams are arranged in line order, starting farthest away from London for all main lines and those branches with junction allowing through running from London. If the junction faces the other way the drawings are arranged from the junction to the terminus.

The quoted opening and closing dates of signal boxes call for some explanation, as it must not be thought that they were necessarily manned continuously over that period. Those boxes fitted with a closing switch were often closed regularly at night or on Sundays, and some were in fact switched out permanently for long periods before their final abolition.
The "opening date" is therefore that on which the equipment was officially brought into use, and the "closing" date indicates when the signals, instruments etc. were removed or made inoperative by the Signal Engineer.

SIGNALS

These are drawn parallel to the track, facing the direction to which they apply. Although the configuration is represented as accurately as possible, no attempt is made to differentiate between tall and short signal posts except in a few cases where these dimensions are extreme.
Signal arms and discs are depicted in the "normal" position - usually at Danger/Caution. Whenever possible, the distance of each running signal from the centre of the controlling signal box is given in yards. Some former SR box diagrams give full distance tables for points and signals.

POINTS

Points controlled from a lever frame or panel are drawn to the split-line format, the position in which they lie when the lever is normal in the frame being shown by the continuous line. Points which do not connect with a running line are often worked by individual hand levers and have no recognised "normal" and "reverse", and are therefore shown differently (see symbols page).

TRACK CIRCUITS & TREADLES

These are either numbered according to function (2AT - signal 2 Approach Track) lettered singly on small layouts (A,B,C, etc.) or lettered in a progressive sequence (AA, AB, AC, BB, BC, etc.).
Where both track circuits and treadles are present, the treadle letters are shown plain and those applying to track circuits enclosed in a circle. In coloured light areas the overlap of each track circuit beyond the signals is given thus: "OL 440".

GROUND FRAMES

Ground Frames are provided to work points, level crossings too far from the signal box for direct observation by the signalman or beyond the distance limit for mechanical operation. Their functions are always released from the controlling signal box, and several methods of doing this are to be found. The most common are the S.R. standard electrical release lever (ELEC REL) and the mechanical release (MECH REL), but Annett's keys were much favoured by the G.W.R.
The lever numbers of ground frames (where known) are written within a distinctive shape - a circle, square, triangle etc. - to avoid confusion with numbers in the main signal box lever frame.

ACKNOWLEDGMENTS

The assistance of several members of the Signalling Record Society, particularly David Collins and John Morris in the preparation of this volume is gratefully acknowledged.

INDEX TO DIAGRAMS IN VOLUME 20

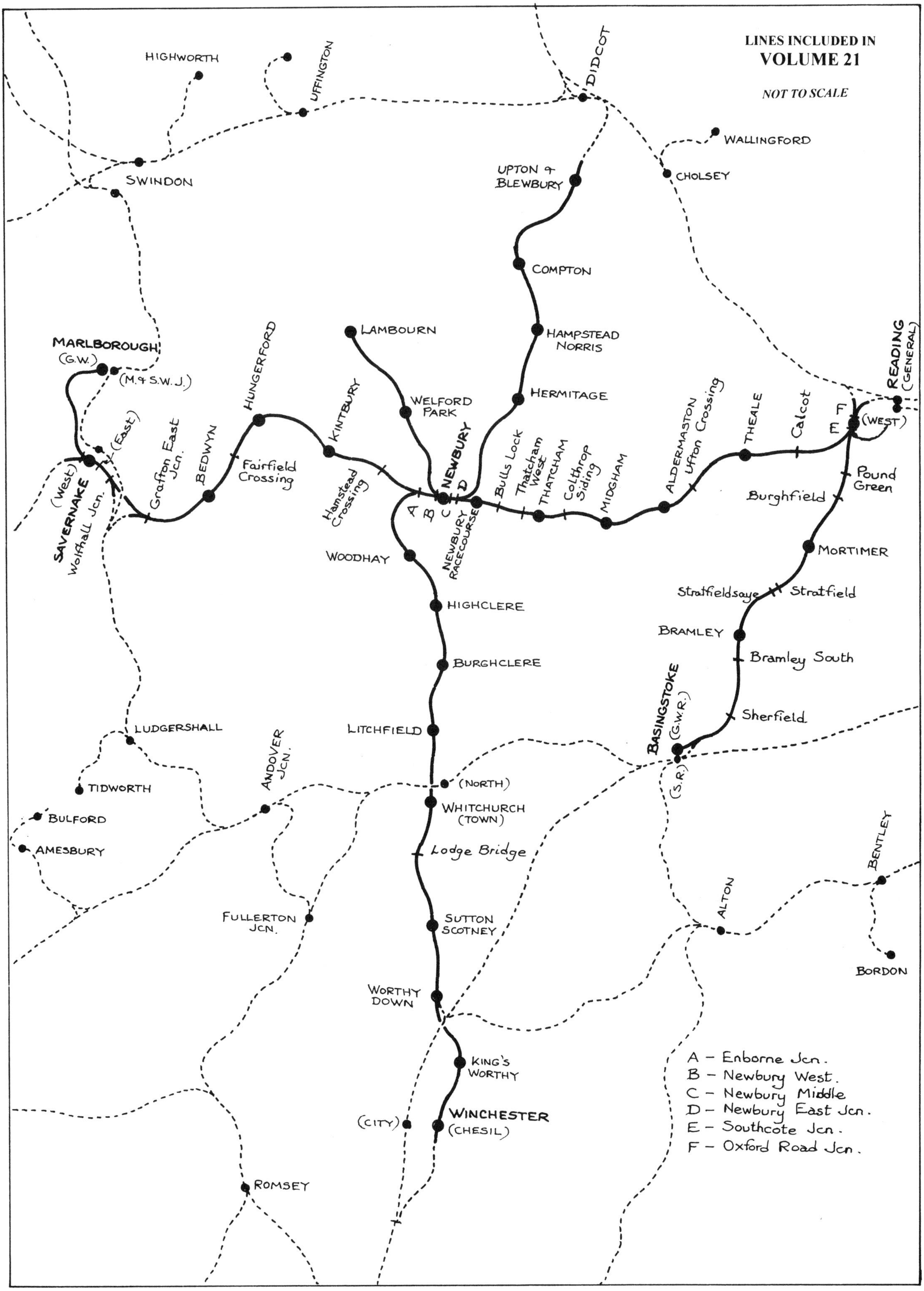
LINES INCLUDED IN
VOLUME 21
NOT TO SCALE
HIGHWORTH
UFFINGTON
DIDCOT
SWINDON
WALLINGFORD
CHOLSEY
UPTON & BLEWBURY
COMPTON
HAMPSTEAD NORRIS
HERMITAGE
LAMBOURN
WELFORD PARK
MARLBOROUGH (G.W.)
(M.& S.W.J.)
(East)
(West)
SAVERNAKE
Wolfhall Jcn.
Grafton East Jcn.
BEDWYN
HUNGERFORD
Fairfield Crossing
KINTBURY
Hamstead Crossing
NEWBURY
A
B
C
D
NEWBURY RACECOURSE
Bulls Lock
Thatcham West
THATCHAM
Colthrop Siding
MIDGHAM
ALDERMASTON
Ufton Crossing
THEALE
Calcot
READING (GENERAL)
F
E
(WEST)
Pound Green
Burghfield
MORTIMER
Stratfieldsaye
Stratfield
BRAMLEY
Bramley South
Sherfield
BASINGSTOKE (G.W.R.)
(S.R.)
WOODHAY
HIGHCLERE
BURGHCLERE
LITCHFIELD
(NORTH)
WHITCHURCH (TOWN)
Lodge Bridge
SUTTON SCOTNEY
WORTHY DOWN
KING'S WORTHY
WINCHESTER (CHESIL)
(CITY)
LUDGERSHALL
TIDWORTH
BULFORD
AMESBURY
ANDOVER JCN.
FULLERTON JCN.
ROMSEY
ALTON
BENTLEY
BORDON
A – Enborne Jcn.
B – Newbury West.
C – Newbury Middle
D – Newbury East Jcn.
E – Southcote Jcn.
F – Oxford Road Jcn.

SECTION ONE

BERKS & HANTS MAIN LINE

(READING TO SAVERNAKE)

LINE OPENED: READING TO HUNGERFORD 21-12-1847.
WEST OF HUNGERFORD 11-11-1862.

UPGRADED TO MAIN LINE STATUS 1900.

SAVERNAKE WEST

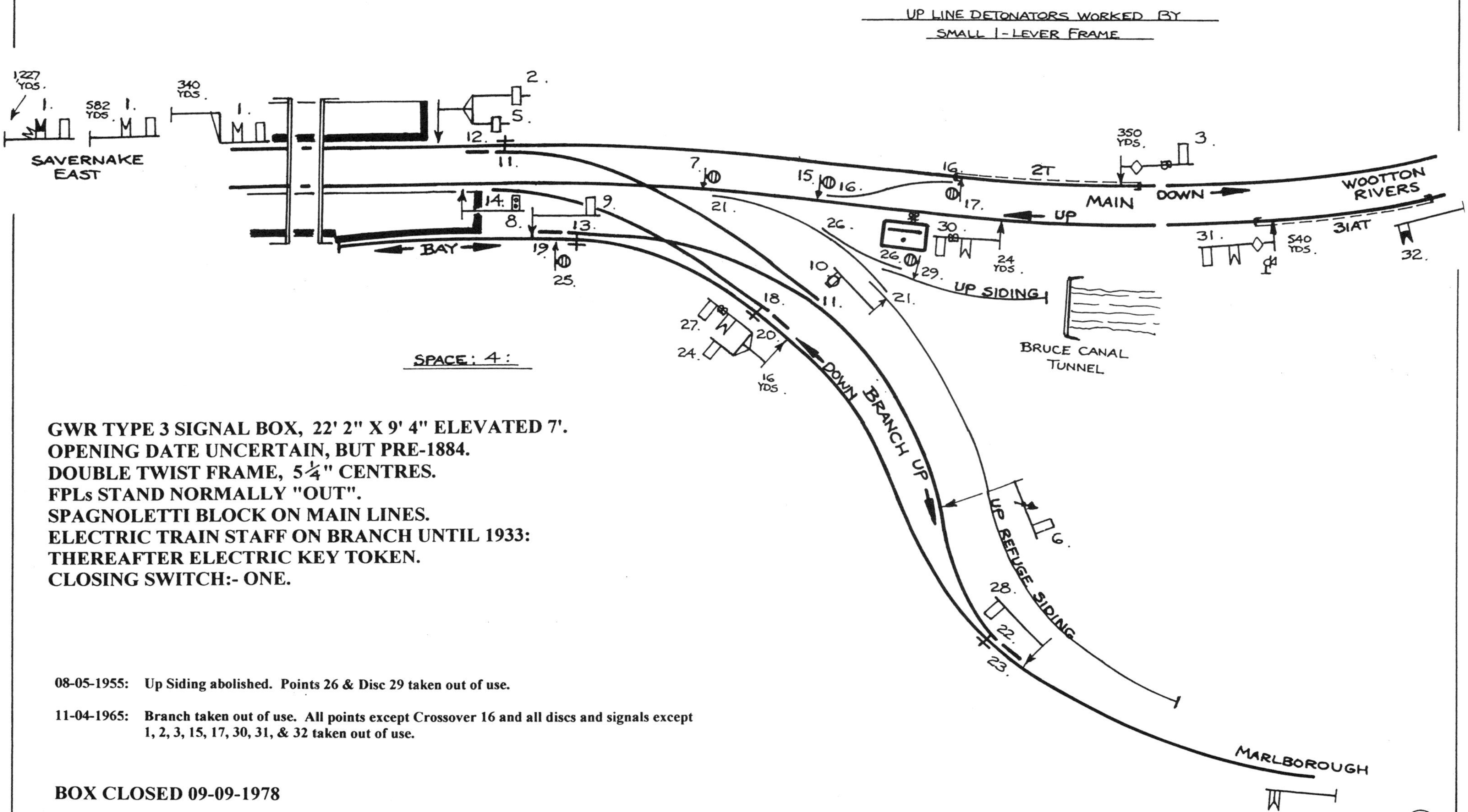

GWR TYPE 3 SIGNAL BOX, 22' 2" X 9' 4" ELEVATED 7'.
OPENING DATE UNCERTAIN, BUT PRE-1884.
DOUBLE TWIST FRAME, 5¼" CENTRES.
FPLs STAND NORMALLY "OUT".
SPAGNOLETTI BLOCK ON MAIN LINES.
ELECTRIC TRAIN STAFF ON BRANCH UNTIL 1933:
THEREAFTER ELECTRIC KEY TOKEN.
CLOSING SWITCH:- ONE.

08-05-1955: Up Siding abolished. Points 26 & Disc 29 taken out of use.

11-04-1965: Branch taken out of use. All points except Crossover 16 and all discs and signals except 1, 2, 3, 15, 17, 30, 31, & 32 taken out of use.

BOX CLOSED 09-09-1978

SAVERNAKE EAST

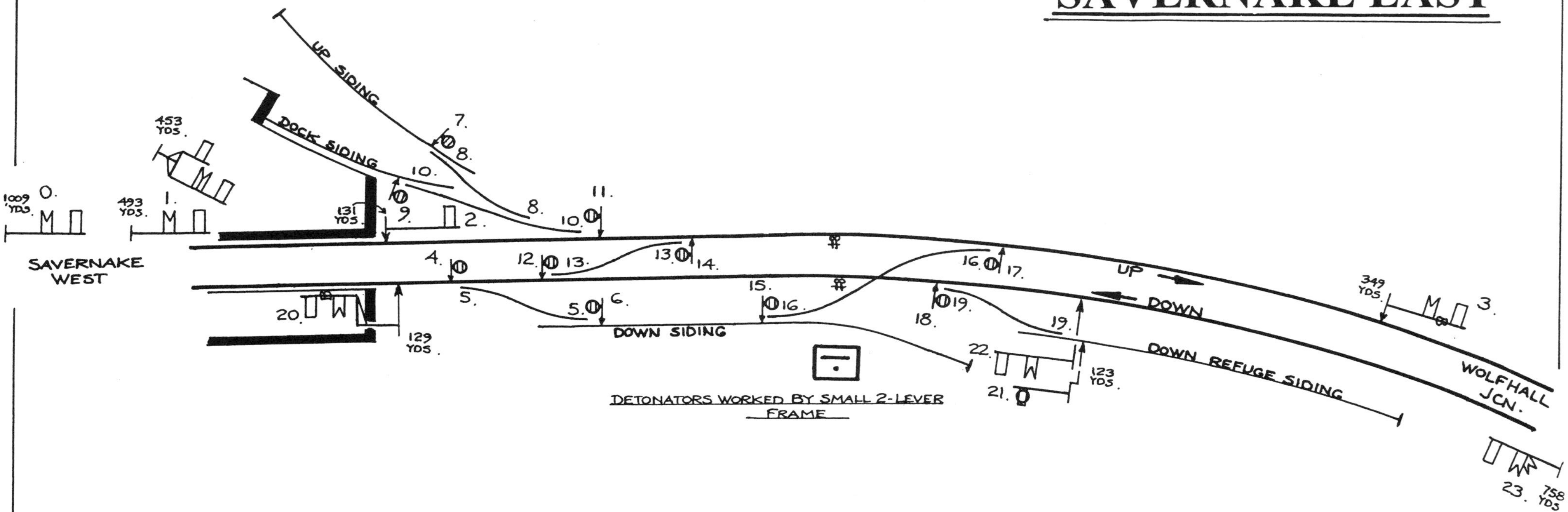

GWR TYPE 3 SIGNAL BOX, OPENING DATE UNCERTAIN, BUT PRE 1884.
DOUBLE TWIST FRAME, 5¼" CENTRES.
SPAGNOLETTI BLOCK.
CLOSING SWITCH:- ONE

23-08-1964: **Down Siding and Down Refuge Siding taken out of use. Points 5, 16, 19, and Discs 4, 6, 15, 17, & 18 and Signal 21 abolished.**

BOX CLOSED 04-12-1968

WOLFHALL JUNCTION

THIS LAYOUT OPERATIVE FROM 1933

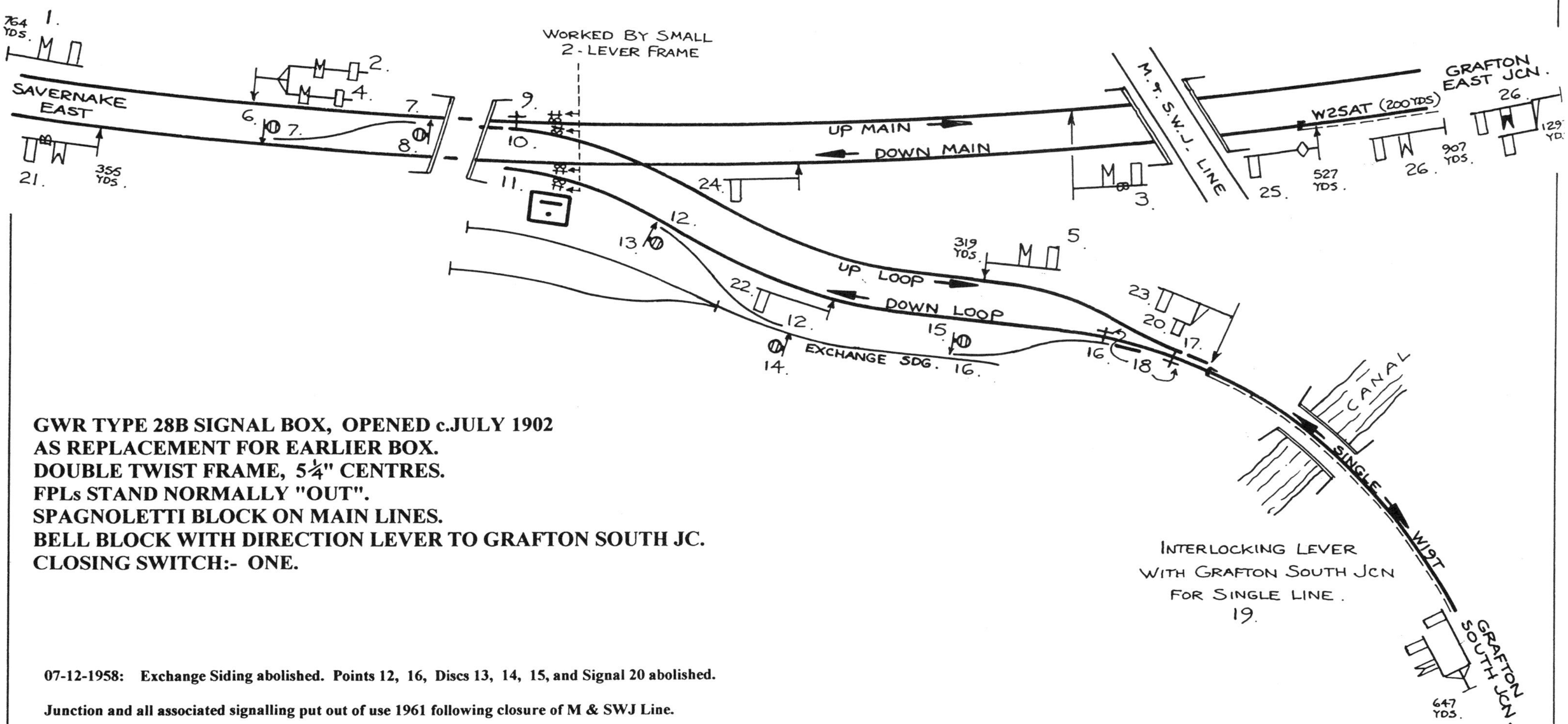

GWR TYPE 28B SIGNAL BOX, OPENED c.JULY 1902
AS REPLACEMENT FOR EARLIER BOX.
DOUBLE TWIST FRAME, 5¼" CENTRES.
FPLs STAND NORMALLY "OUT".
SPAGNOLETTI BLOCK ON MAIN LINES.
BELL BLOCK WITH DIRECTION LEVER TO GRAFTON SOUTH JC.
CLOSING SWITCH:- ONE.

07-12-1958: Exchange Siding abolished. Points 12, 16, Discs 13, 14, 15, and Signal 20 abolished.

Junction and all associated signalling put out of use 1961 following closure of M & SWJ Line.

BOX CLOSED 22-11-1964.

GRAFTON EAST JUNCTION

"GRAFTON CURVE" UNTIL 06-03-1933

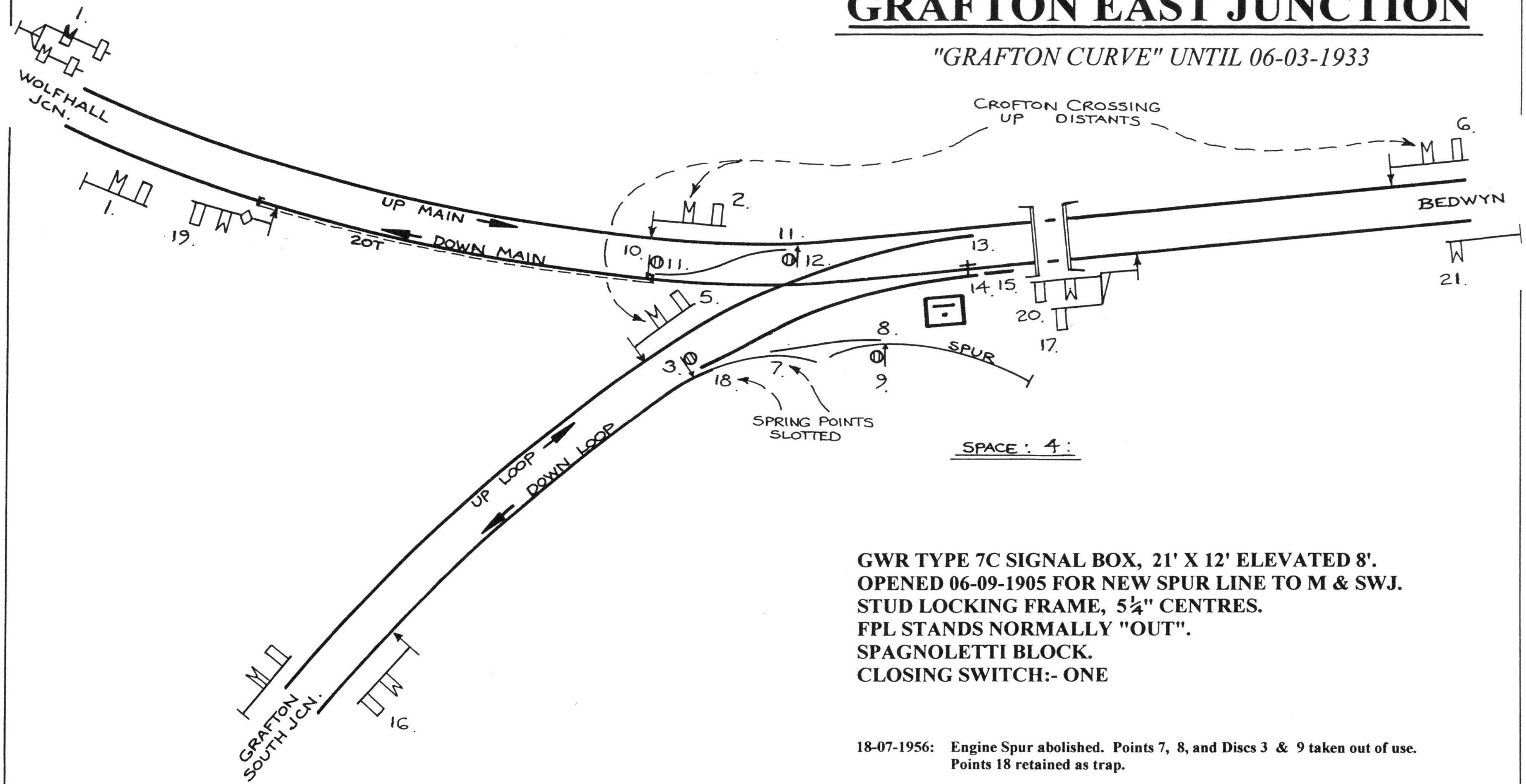

GWR TYPE 7C SIGNAL BOX, 21' X 12' ELEVATED 8'.
OPENED 06-09-1905 FOR NEW SPUR LINE TO M & SWJ.
STUD LOCKING FRAME, 5¼" CENTRES.
FPL STANDS NORMALLY "OUT".
SPAGNOLETTI BLOCK.
CLOSING SWITCH:- ONE

18-07-1956: Engine Spur abolished. Points 7, 8, and Discs 3 & 9 taken out of use. Points 18 retained as trap.

05-05-1957: Loop Lines and Crossover taken out of use. All levers except 1, 2, 6, 19, 20, and 21 then spare.

BOX CLOSED 22-11-1964

BEDWYN

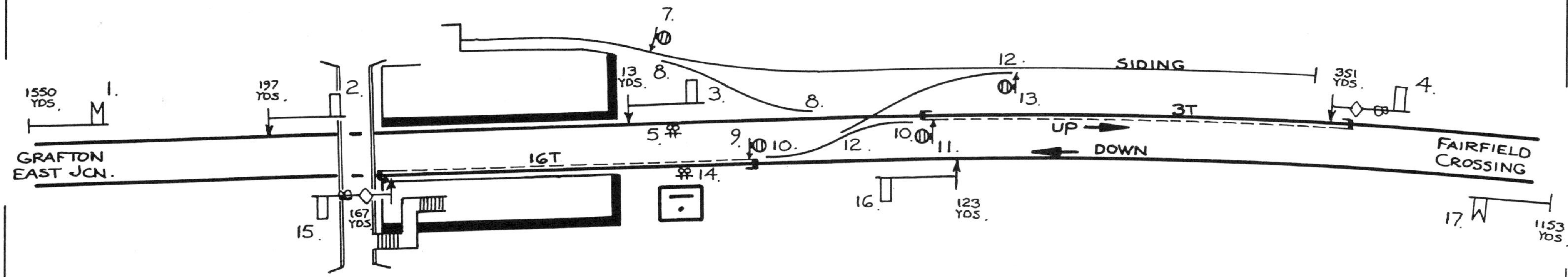

SPACE : 6 :

GWR TYPE 7A SIGNAL BOX, 21' X 12' ELEVATED 8'.
OPENED 1897 AS REPLACEMENT FOR ORIGINAL.
DOUBLE TWIST FRAME, 5¼" CENTRES.
SPAGNOLETTI BLOCK, LATER WR 3-POSITION.
CLOSING SWITCH:- ONE.

19-09-1965: Layout altered. Slip Points 12 and Crossover 10 abolished and Points 8 moved eastward to position Fairfield Crossing side of previous No. 12 Points. Crossover 10 renewed opposite signal box.

BOX CLOSED 11-09-1978.

FAIRFIELD CROSSING

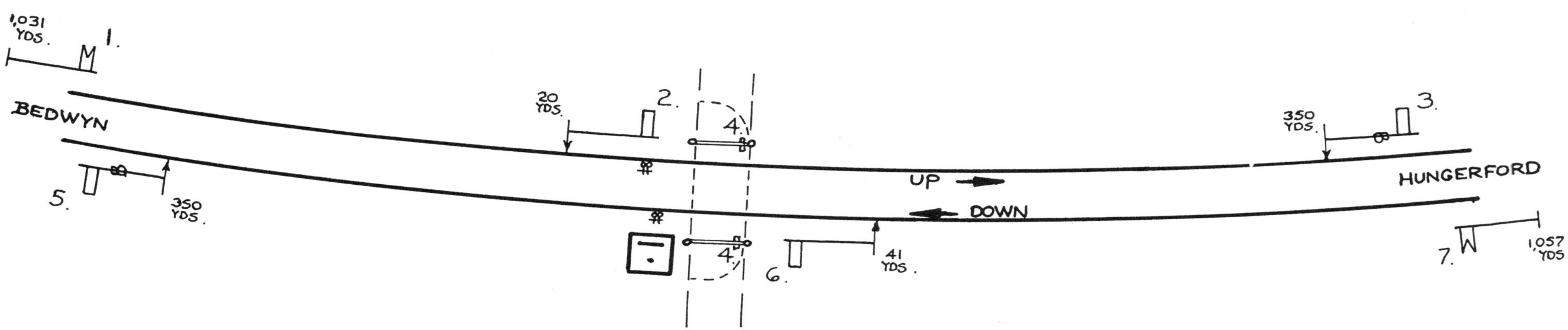

DETONATORS WORKED BY SMALL 2-LEVER FRAME.

GWR TYPE 28B SIGNAL BOX, 12' 6" X 10'.
OPENED 06-06-1907 AS REPLACEMENT FOR ORIGINAL.
STUD LOCKING FRAME, 5¼" CENTRES.
GATES WORKED BY HAND.
SPAGNOLETTI BLOCK.
CLOSING SWITCH:- ONE.

BOX OFFICIALLY CLOSED 07-03-1951. SIGNALS AND BOX STRUCTURE REMOVED 28-04-1957.

HUNGERFORD (1950)

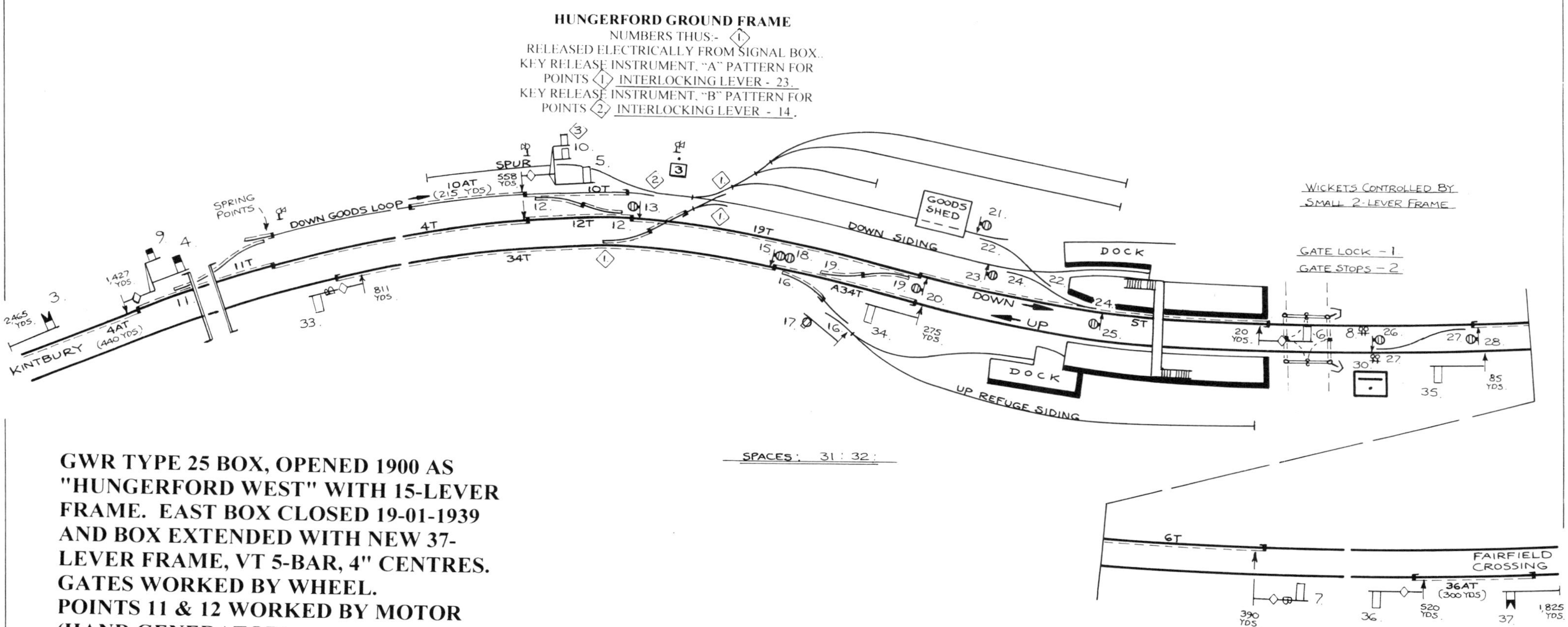

GWR TYPE 25 BOX, OPENED 1900 AS "HUNGERFORD WEST" WITH 15-LEVER FRAME. EAST BOX CLOSED 19-01-1939 AND BOX EXTENDED WITH NEW 37-LEVER FRAME, VT 5-BAR, 4" CENTRES.
GATES WORKED BY WHEEL.
POINTS 11 & 12 WORKED BY MOTOR (HAND GENERATOR).
SPAGNOLETTI BLOCK, LATER WR 3-POSITION.
CLOSING SWITCH:- ONE.

BOX DESTROYED BY DERAILMENT 10-11-1971. TEMPY. BOX IN USE FROM 11-11-1971 UNTIL 19-03-1972. SEE NEXT PAGE FOR PERMANENT REPLACEMENT.

HUNGERFORD (1973)

**BR (W) TYPE 37B SIGNAL BOX,
39' X 13' ELEVATED 12, PARTS
SECOND HAND EX BRISTOL EAST
DEPOT MAIN LINE.
OPENED 19-02-1972 AS PERMANENT
REPLACEMENT FOR DAMAGED BOX.
VT 5-BAR FRAME, 4" CENTRES.
WR 3-POSITION BLOCK.
ILLUMINATED DIAGRAM.
CLOSING SWITCH:- NIL.
GATES WORKED BY WHEEL.
POINTS 26 & 27 WORKED BY MOTOR
(HAND GENERATOR).**

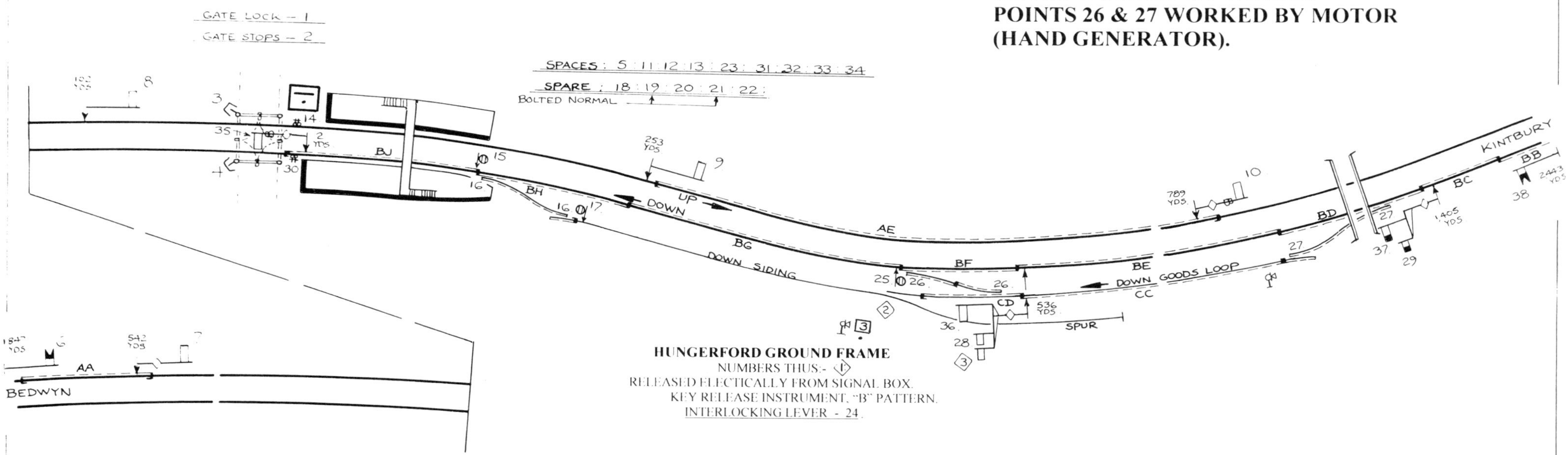

29-07-1973: Down Siding terminated in buffer stops at point opposite N0. 9 Signal, and Points 16 & Discs 15 and 17 abolished.

BOX CLOSED 17-07-1978. AREA THEN CONTROLLED BY READING PANEL.

KINTBURY

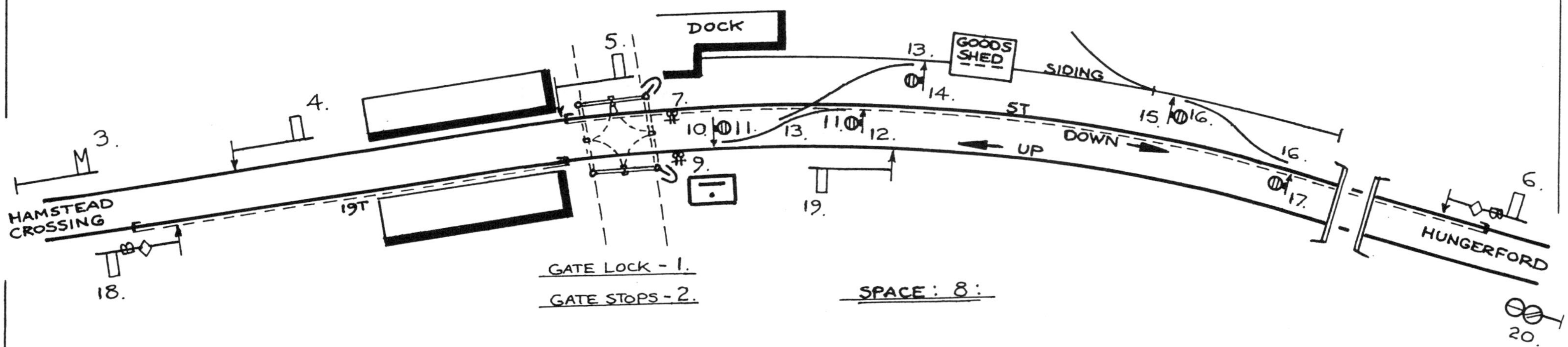

GWR SIGNAL BOX OF UNCONFIRMED TYPE,
OPENED BY 1884 AND REBUILT 1947.
STUD LOCKING FRAME, 4" CENTRES, INSTALLED 1912.
GATES WORKED BY WHEEL.
SPAGNOLETTI BLOCK, LATER WR 3-POSITION.
CLOSING SWITCH:- NIL.

20-10-1963: Points 11, 13, and Discs 10, 12. & 14 taken out of use.
Remaining Siding connection (16) and associated Discs abolished 1965.

04-10-1971: Level Crossing Gates replaced by Full Lifting Barriers.

BOX CLOSED 16-04-1978

HAMSTEAD CROSSING

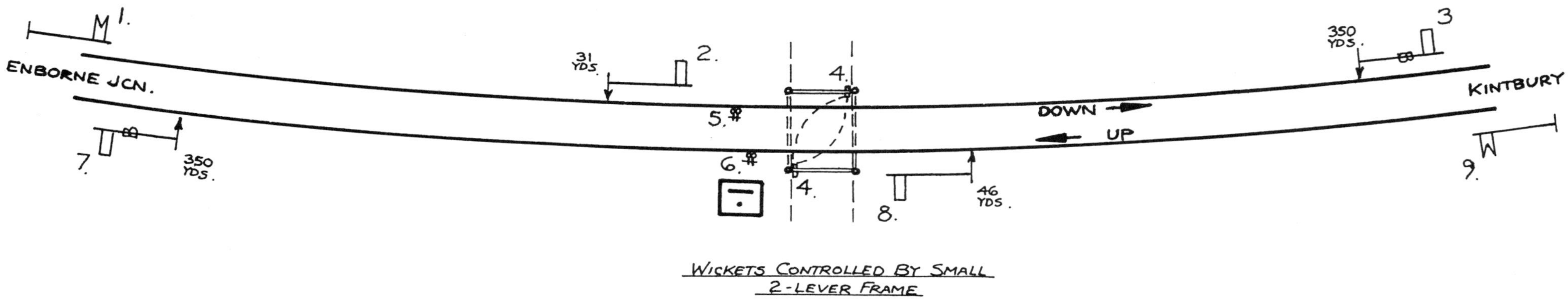

GWR NON-STANDARD SIGNAL BOX, 17' X 11' ELEVATED 8'.
OPENED 09-03-1921 TO REPLACE ORIGINAL.
STUD LOCKING FRAME, 5¼" CENTRES.
GATES WORKED BY HAND.
SPAGNOLETTI BLOCK.
CLOSING SWITCH:- NIL.

BOX CLOSED 15-07-1978

ENBORNE JUNCTION (1944)

THIS LAYOUT OPERATIVE FROM JULY 1943. LINE TO WOODHAY DOUBLED 06-12-1942 AND UP GOODS LOOP ADDED 13-07-1943.

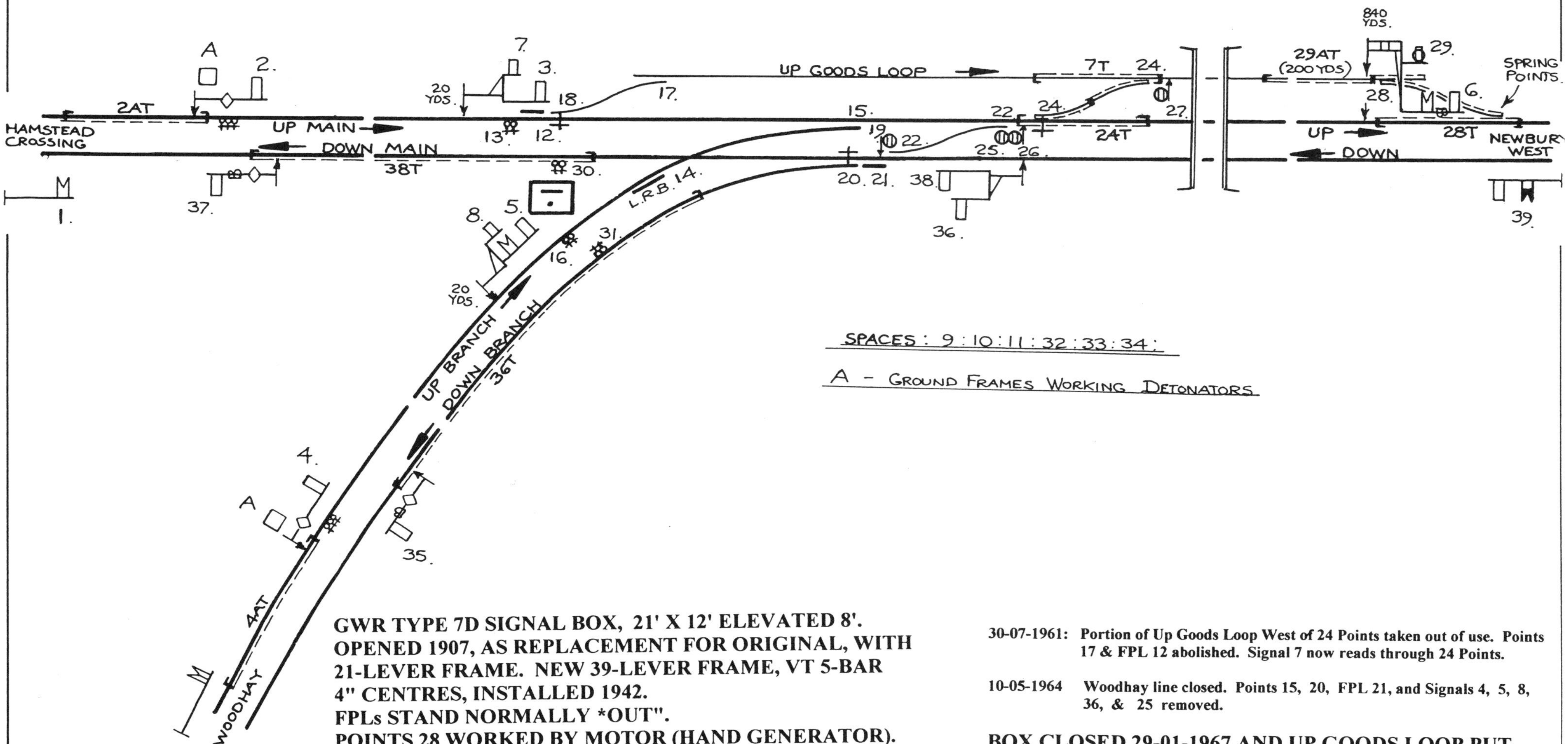

GWR TYPE 7D SIGNAL BOX, 21' X 12' ELEVATED 8'.
OPENED 1907, AS REPLACEMENT FOR ORIGINAL, WITH 21-LEVER FRAME. NEW 39-LEVER FRAME, VT 5-BAR 4" CENTRES, INSTALLED 1942.
FPLs STAND NORMALLY *OUT".
POINTS 28 WORKED BY MOTOR (HAND GENERATOR).
SPAGNOLETTI BLOCK.
CLOSING SWITCH:- ONE (ON MAIN LINES).

30-07-1961: Portion of Up Goods Loop West of 24 Points taken out of use. Points 17 & FPL 12 abolished. Signal 7 now reads through 24 Points.

10-05-1964 Woodhay line closed. Points 15, 20, FPL 21, and Signals 4, 5, 8, 36, & 25 removed.

BOX CLOSED 29-01-1967 AND UP GOODS LOOP PUT OUT OF USE.

NEWBURY WEST

GWR TYPE 7D SIGNAL BOX, 33' 6" X 12' ELEVATED 11'.
OPENED 1910 TO REPLACE ORIGINAL.
HT 3-BAR FRAME, 4" CENTRES.
FPLs STAND NORMALLY "OUT".
SPAGNOLETTI BLOCK ON MAIN AND PLATFORM LINES, LATER REPLACED WITH WR 3-POSITION.
ELECTRIC KEY TOKEN TO WELFORD PARK UNTIL 01-07-1962, THEN "ONE TRAIN" WORKING WITH WOODEN STAFF.
CLOSING SWITCH:- ONE (VIA PLATFORMS).

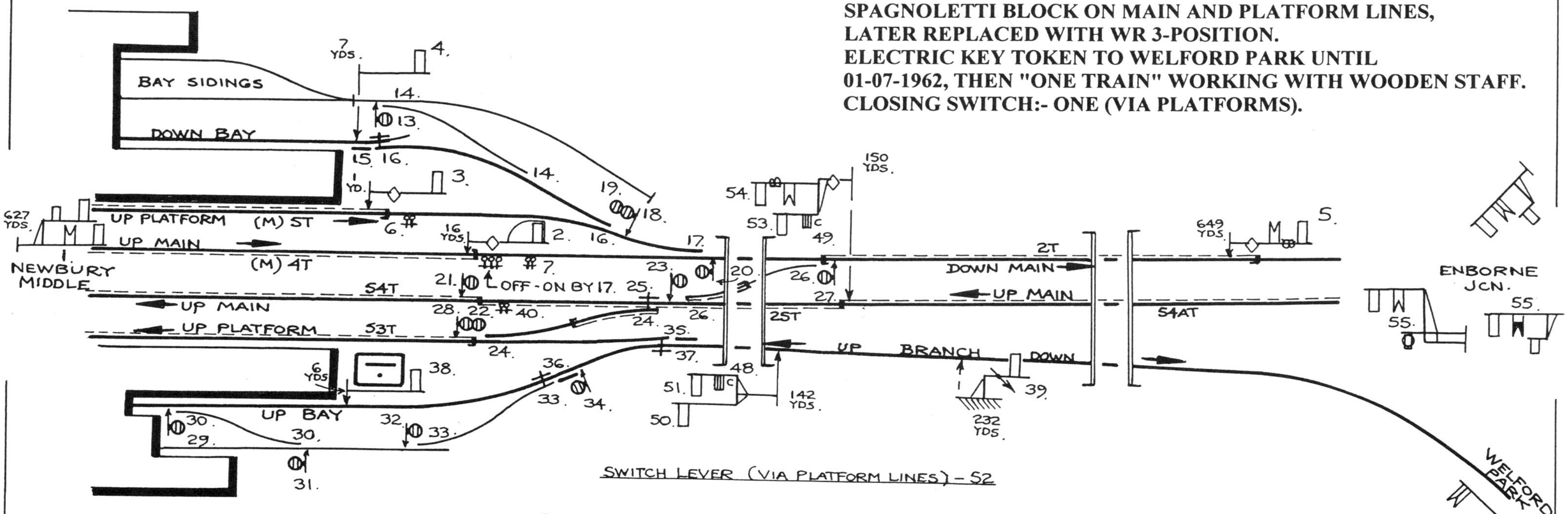

SWITCH LEVER (VIA PLATFORM LINES) - 52

SPACES : 8 : 9 : 10 : 11 : 12 : 41 : 42 : 43 : 44 : 45 : 46 : 47 :

03-07-1962: Points 30, 33, FPL 36, Discs 29, 31, 32, & 34 taken out of use.

24-10-1965: Up Bay abolished. Points 35 retained as trap. Signals 38, 38, & 50 removed. Signal 51 fitted with 3' arm.

BOX CLOSED 16-04-1978. AREA THEN CONTROLLED BY READING PANEL.

NEWBURY MIDDLE

GWR TYPE 7D SIGNAL BOX,
29' X 11' ELEVATED 9'.
OPENED JUNE 1910 TO REPLACE OLD BOX.
HT 3-BAR FRAME, 4" CENTRES.
FPLs STAND NORMALLY "OUT".
SPAGNOLETTI BLOCK.
CLOSING SWITCH:- ONE.

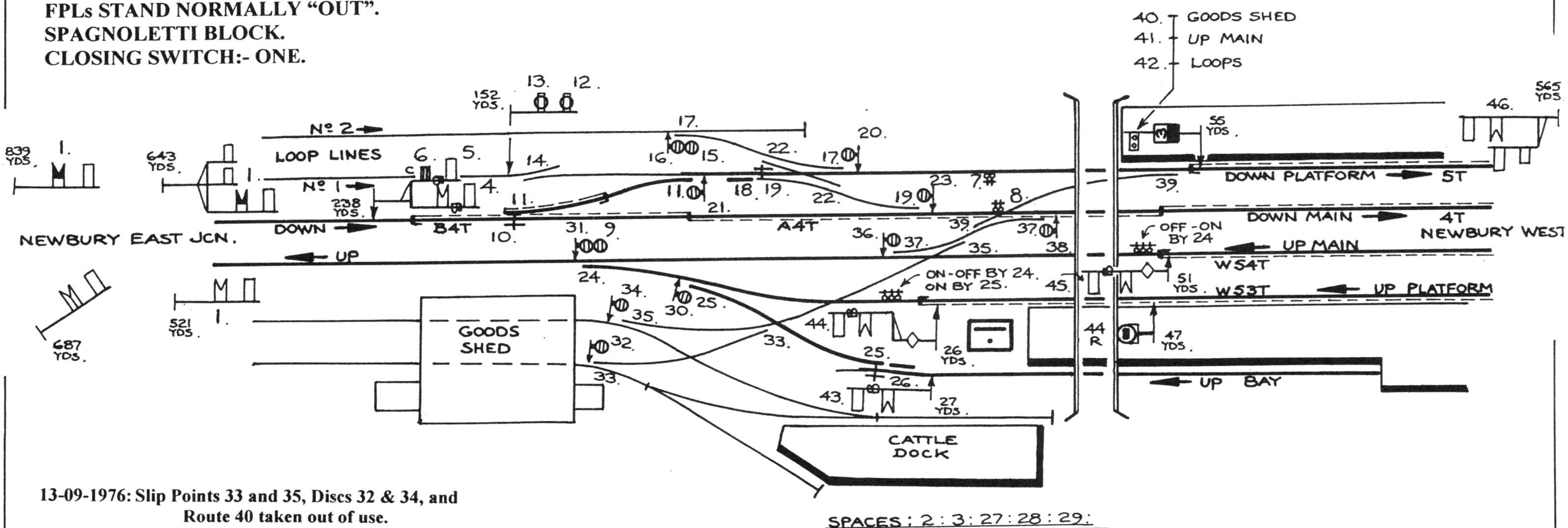

13-09-1976: Slip Points 33 and 35, Discs 32 & 34, and Route 40 taken out of use.

26-02-1978: No. 1 Loop and portion of Down Platform Line taken out of use. Points 11, 14, 19, 22, 39, FPLs 10, 18, Signals 5, 6, 12, 13, & 41/42, and all associated Discs abolished. Points 17 secured in "Reverse" position, and access to Down Platform Line available only from East Junction Box via No. 2 Loop.

BOX CLOSED 04-03-1978.

NEWBURY EAST JCN.

GWR TYPE 7C SIGNAL BOX,
50' X 14' X 11', OPENED 1908.
HT 3-BAR FRAME, 5¼" CENTRES.
CONVERTED TO 5-BAR LOCKING 1948.
FPLs STAND NORMALLY "OUT".
SPAGNOLETTI BLOCK ON MAIN LINES AND BRANCH.

PERMISSIVE BLOCK TO MIDDLE BOX OVER 1 & 2 LOOP LINES.
CLOSING SWITCH:- ONE.

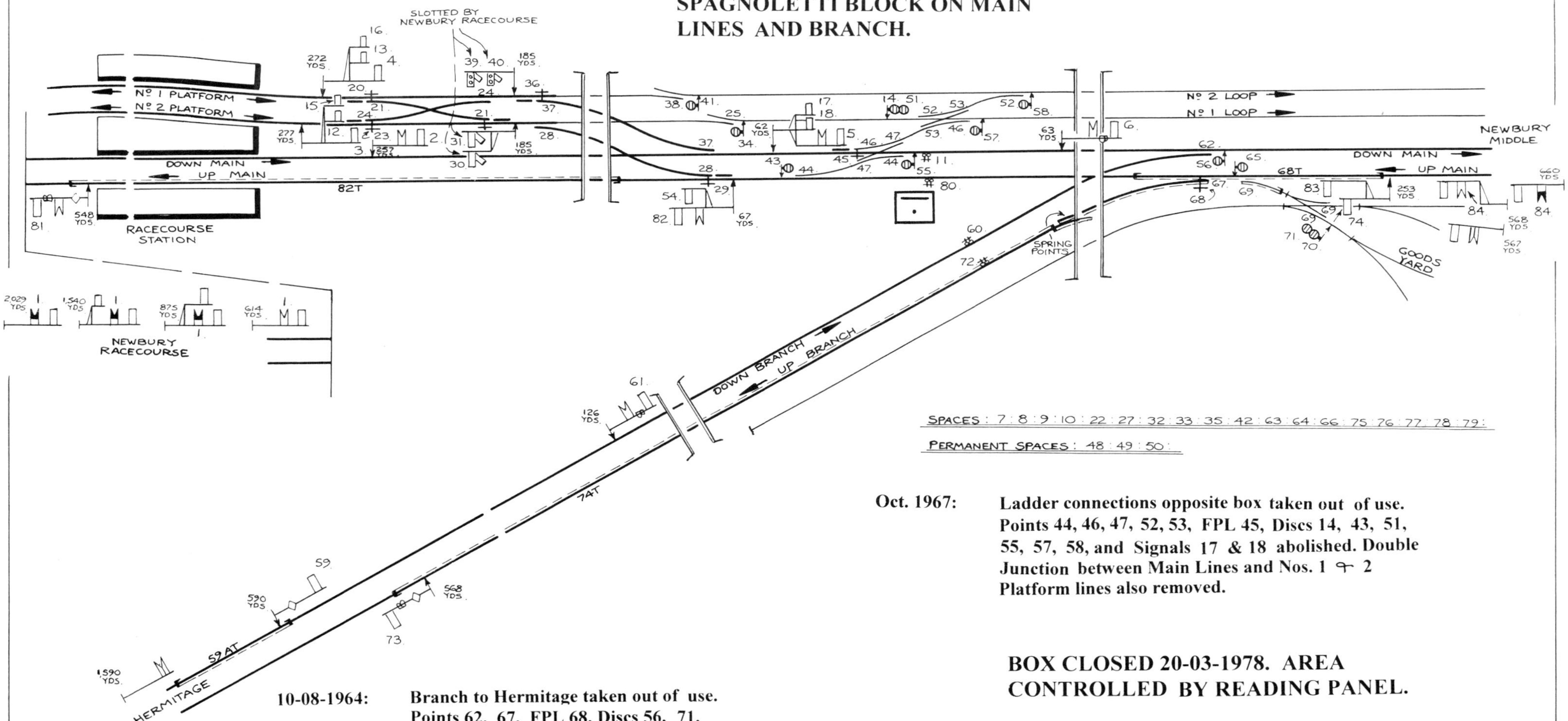

SPACES : 7 : 8 : 9 : 10 : 22 : 27 : 32 : 33 : 35 : 42 : 63 : 64 : 66 : 75 : 76 : 77 : 78 : 79 :

PERMANENT SPACES : 48 : 49 : 50 :

Oct. 1967: Ladder connections opposite box taken out of use. Points 44, 46, 47, 52, 53, FPL 45, Discs 14, 43, 51, 55, 57, 58, and Signals 17 & 18 abolished. Double Junction between Main Lines and Nos. 1 & 2 Platform lines also removed.

BOX CLOSED 20-03-1978. AREA CONTROLLED BY READING PANEL.

10-08-1964: Branch to Hermitage taken out of use. Points 62, 67, FPL 68, Discs 56, 71, Detonators 60, 72, and Signals 59, 61, 73 & 74 abolished.

NEWBURY RACECOURSE

THIS LAYOUT OPERATIVE FROM 23-11-1962,
WHEN SHELL MEX & BP SIDING BROUGHT INTO USE.

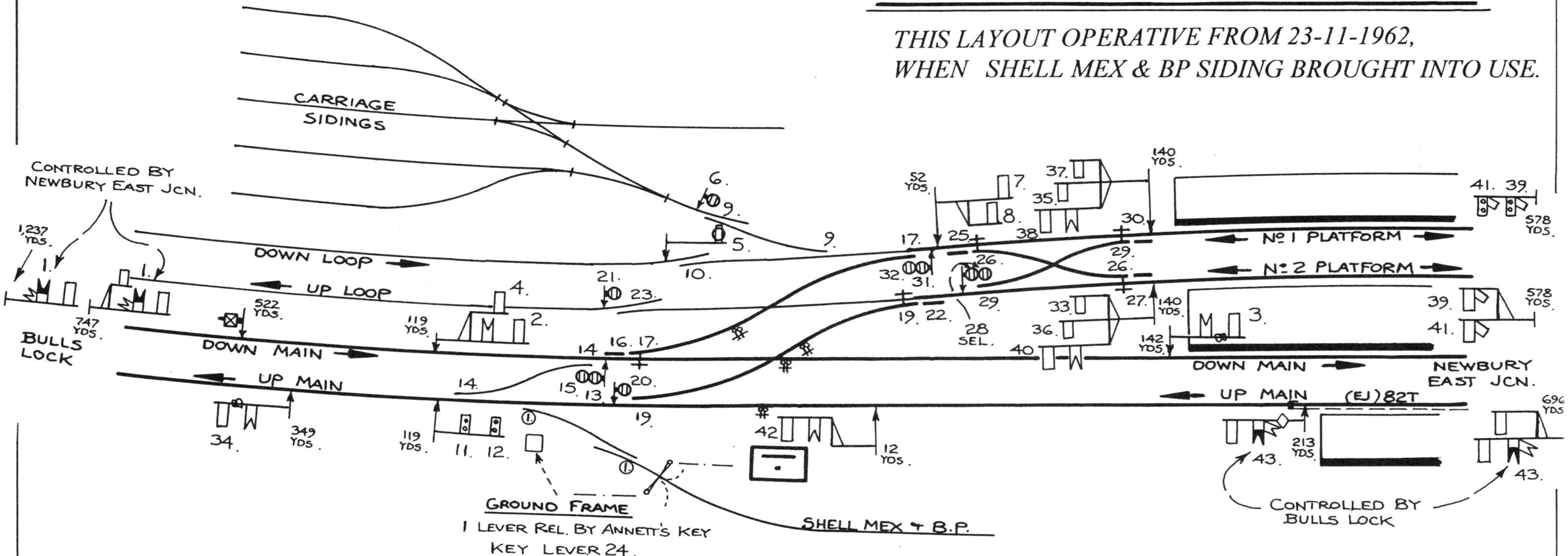

04-08-1963: Loop Lines from Bulls Lock taken out of use and permissive instrument recovered. Points 10, 23, Disc 21, and Signals 5, 35, & 36 abolished. "A" end of Points 9 secured in "Reverse" position.

SPACE : 18 :

DETONATORS WORKED BY SMALL 2-LEVER FRAME.

GWR TYPE 27C SIGNAL BOX, OPENED 1905 AS "NEWBURY RACECOURSE EAST". RENAMED 1910. DOUBLE TWIST FRAME, 5¼" CENTRES, LATER CONVERTED TO 5-BAR VT LOCKING.

FPLs SRAND NORMALLY "OUT".

SPAGNOLETTI BLOCK ON MAIN LINES, LATER WR 3-POSITION.

PERMISSIVE BLOCK TO BULLS LOCK ON LOOP LINES.

CLOSING SWITCH:- ONE.

31-02-1968: Junction between Main and Platform Lines singled. Points 26, FPLs 25, 27, and Signals 8 & 33 abolished.

BOX CLOSED 16-01-1978. AREA THEN CONTROLLED BY READING PANEL.

BULLS LOCK

Depot Sidings removed c.1950. Points 13, 17, Discs 16, 19, and Signals 12 & 18 removed.

04-08-1963: Up & Down Goods Lines taken out of use and Permissive instrument recovered. Levers 4, 10, 11, 14, 15, and 25 made spare.

BOX CLOSED 26-09-1965

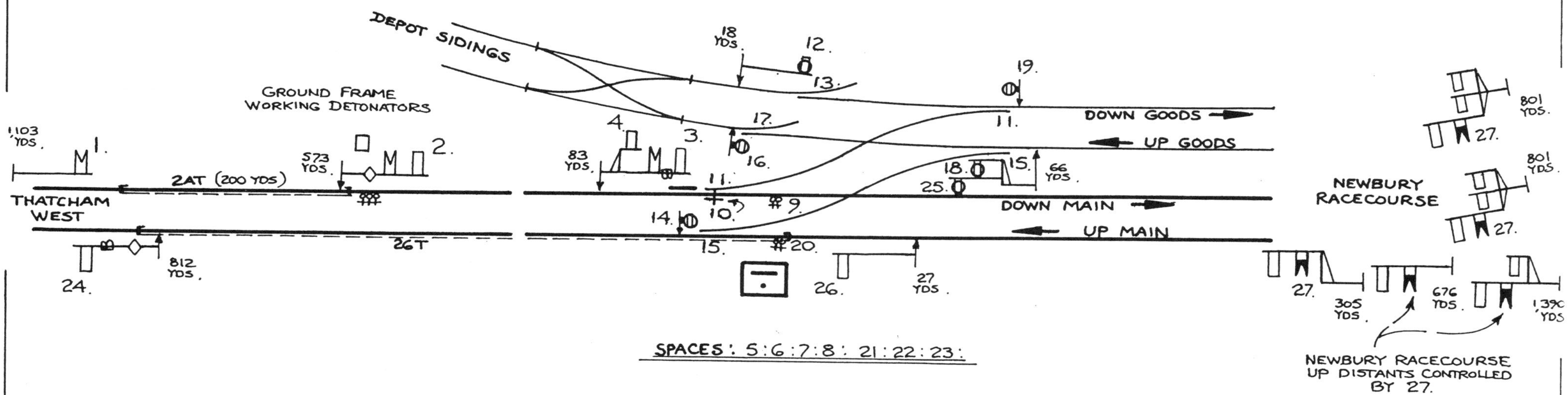

GWR TYPE 13 SIGNAL BOX, 24' 2" X 12' ELEVATED 8'.
OPENED 03-02-1943.
VT 5-BAR FRAME, 4" CENTRES.
FPL STANDS NORMALLY "OUT".
SPAGNOLETTI BLOCK ON MAIN LINES.
PERMISSIVE BLOCK ON GOODS LINES.
CLOSING SWITCH:- ONE.

THATCHAM WEST

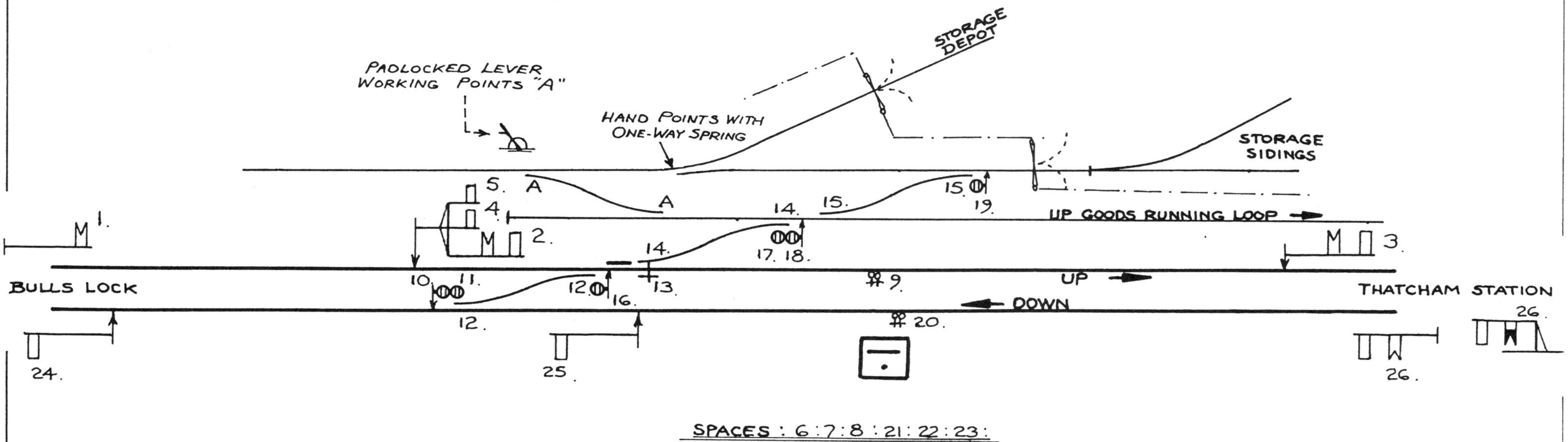

GWR BOX OF UNCONFIRMED TYPE, 25' 2" X 12' 1"
ELEVATED 8'.
OPENED 19-07-1940 FOR NEW GOVERNMENT DEPOT SIDINGS.
VT 5-BAR FRAME, 4" CENTRES, 26 LEVERS.
FPL STANDS NORMALLY "OUT".
SPAGNOLETTI BLOCK ON MAIN LINES.
PERMISSIVE BLOCK TO THATCHAM ON GOODS LOOP.
CLOSING SWITCH:- ONE.

BOX CLOSED 02-01-1966 AND ALL CONNECTIONS ABOLISHED. UP GOODS LINE CONVERTED TO SIDING WITH ACCESS ONLY FROM THATCHAM STATION END.

THATCHAM (1942)

19-11-1967: Portion of Down Siding over Level Crossing abolished. Points 32, Wheel Stop 24, and Discs 22, 25, & 26 taken out of use.

01-11-1976: Down Sidings taken out of use. Points 18, 28, and Discs 17, 27, & 29 abolished.

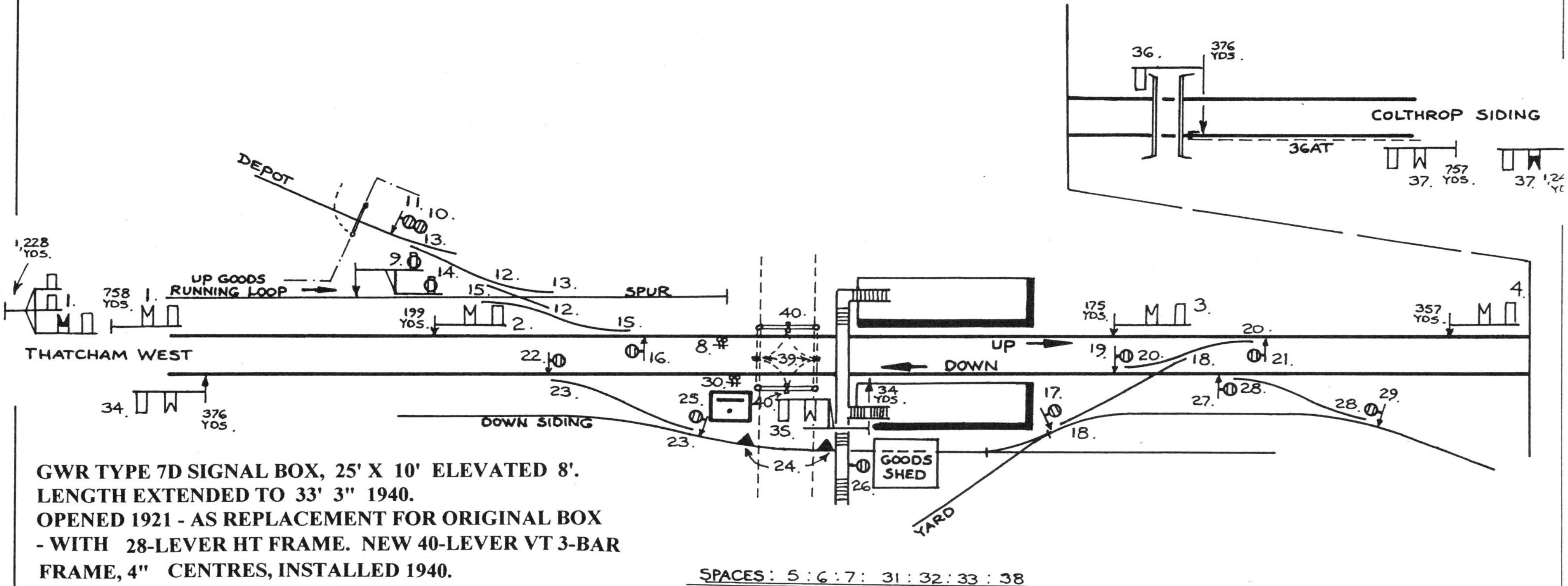

SPACES: 5 : 6 : 7 : 31 : 32 : 33 : 38

GWR TYPE 7D SIGNAL BOX, 25' X 10' ELEVATED 8'.
LENGTH EXTENDED TO 33' 3" 1940.
OPENED 1921 - AS REPLACEMENT FOR ORIGINAL BOX - WITH 28-LEVER HT FRAME. NEW 40-LEVER VT 3-BAR FRAME, 4" CENTRES, INSTALLED 1940.
GATES WORKED BY WHEEL.
SPAGNOLETTI BLOCK ON MAIN LINES, LATER WR 3-POSITION.
PERMISSIVE BLOCK FROM THATCHAM WEST ON GOODS LOOP.
CLOSING SWITCH:- NIL.

02-01-1966: In connection with abolition of Thatcham West Box, Up Goods Running Loop converted to siding and permissive instrument recovered.

06-12-1977: Crossover 20 and Discs 19 & 21 taken out of use.

BOX CLOSED 16-01-1978. GROUND FRAME PROVIDED TO WORK FORMER No. 15 AND 12b POINTS. 12a AND 13a CONVERTED TO HAND OPERATION AND TRAP POINTS 13b ABOLISHED. LEVEL CROSSING CONTROLLED FROM COLTHROP (CCTV).

COLTHROP SIDING (1950)

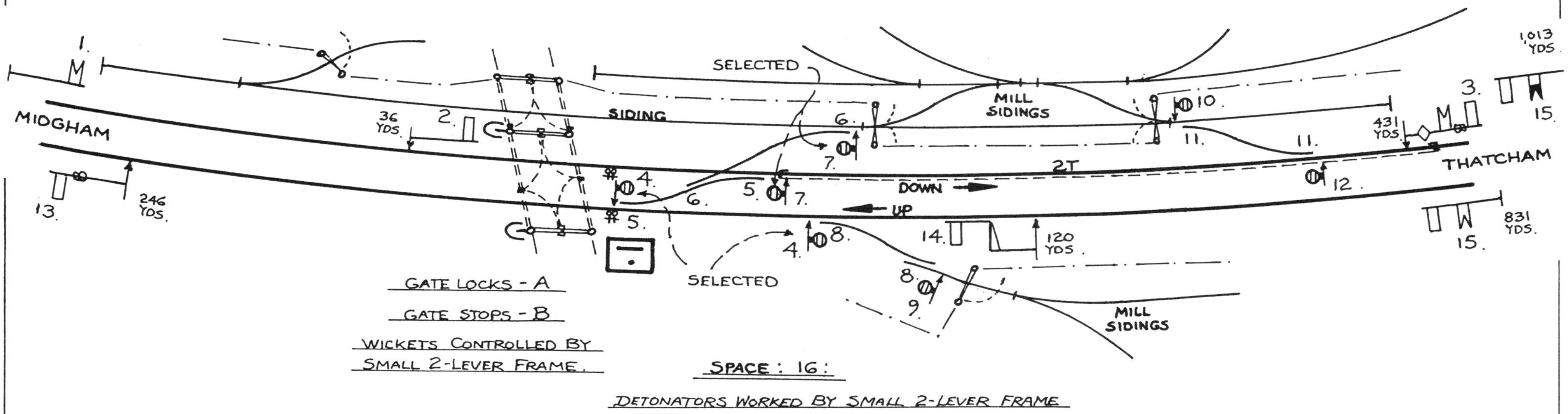

GWR TYPE 7C SIGNAL BOX, 20' 9" X 11' 8"
ELEVATED 8', PARTS SECOND HAND EX SHIFNAL.
OPENED 1912 AS REPLACEMENT FOR ORIGINAL.
STUD LOCKING FRAME, 5¼" CENTRES. LEVERS "A" AND "B" ADDED AND FRAME CONVERTED TO 5-BAR LOCKING 1943.
GATES WORKED BY WHEEL.
SPAGNOLETTI BLOCK, LATER WR 3-POSITION.
CLOSING SWITCH:- ONE.

08-07-1971: Points 11 and Discs 10 & 12 taken out of use.

April 1973: Points 5, 6, and Discs 4a (Selected) and 7 Selected (both) abolished.

22-02-1977: Gates replaced by FLBs.

BOX REDUCED TO GROUND FRAME STATUS 16-01-1978.

MIDGHAM

GWR TYPE 7A SIGNAL BOX, 25' 1" X 12' 1" ELVATED 8'.
OPENED 1898 TO REPLACE ORIGINAL BOX.
DOUBLE TWIST FRAME, 5¼" CENTRES.
GATES WORKED BY WHEEL.
SPAGNOLETTI BLOCK, LATER WR 3-POSITION.
CLOSING SWITCH:- NIL

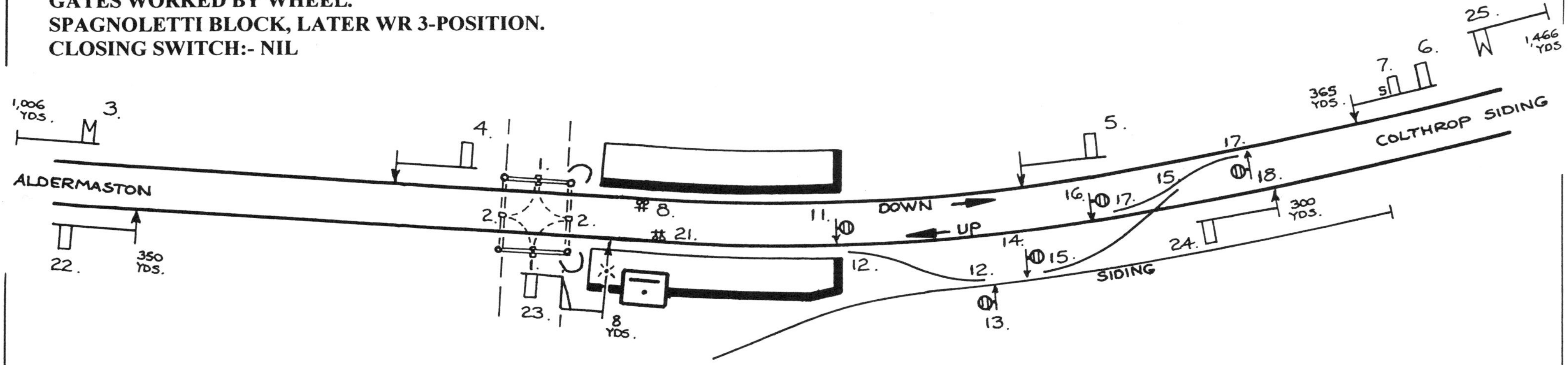

SPACES : 9 : 10 : 19 : 20 :

11-09-1960: All Points and Discs taken out of use.

30-08-1974: Level Crossing gates replaced by FLBs.

BOX CLOSED 05-12-1977. CROSSING THEN CONTROLLED FROM COLTHROP (CCTV).

ALDERMASTON (1944)

THIS LAYOUT OPERATIVE FROM 1943, WHEN UP AND DOWN GOODS LOOPS BROUGHT INTO USE.

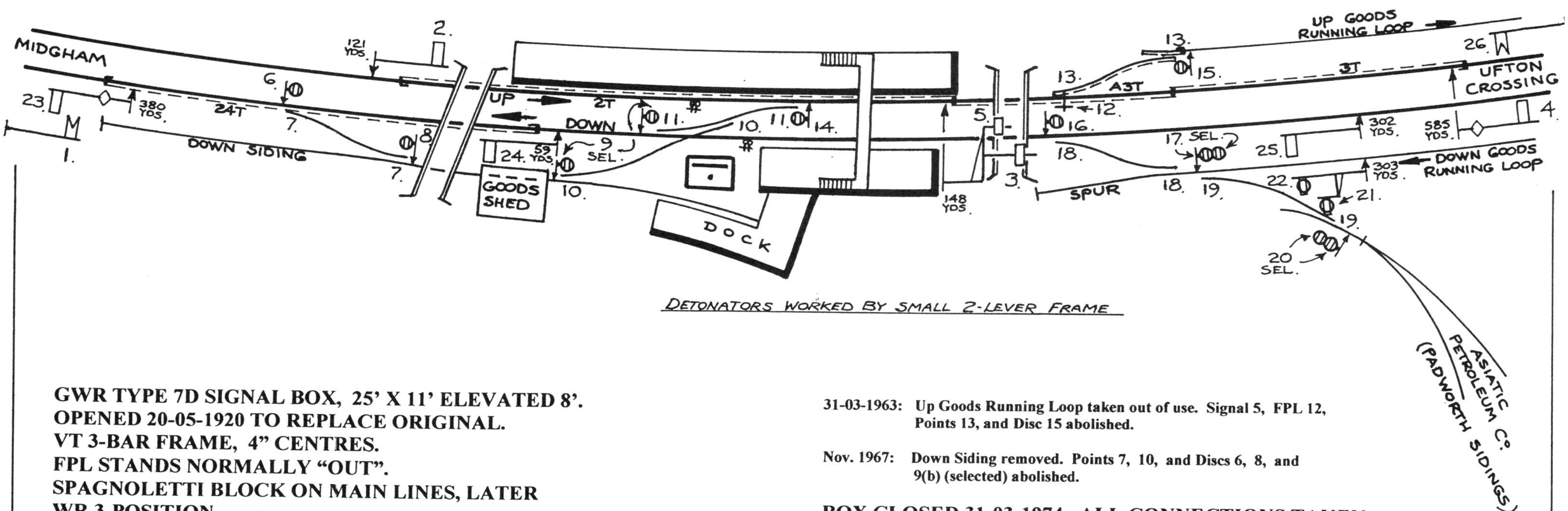

GWR TYPE 7D SIGNAL BOX, 25' X 11' ELEVATED 8'.
OPENED 20-05-1920 TO REPLACE ORIGINAL.
VT 3-BAR FRAME, 4" CENTRES.
FPL STANDS NORMALLY "OUT".
SPAGNOLETTI BLOCK ON MAIN LINES, LATER WR 3-POSITION.
PERMISSIVE BLOCK TO UFTON CROSSING ON GOODS RUNNING LOOPS.
CLOSING SWITCH:- ONE.

31-03-1963: **Up Goods Running Loop taken out of use. Signal 5, FPL 12, Points 13, and Disc 15 abolished.**

Nov. 1967: **Down Siding removed. Points 7, 10, and Discs 6, 8, and 9(b) (selected) abolished.**

BOX CLOSED 31-03-1974. ALL CONNECTIONS TAKEN OUT OF USE, BUT ACCESS TO PADWORTH SIDINGS MAINTAINED BY HAND POINTS IN FORMER DOWN GOODS RUNNING LOOP WITH HEADSHUNT EXTENDED BEHIND DOWN PLATFORM. CONNECTION WITH MAIN LINE AT UFTON CROSSING.

UFTON CROSSING (1944)

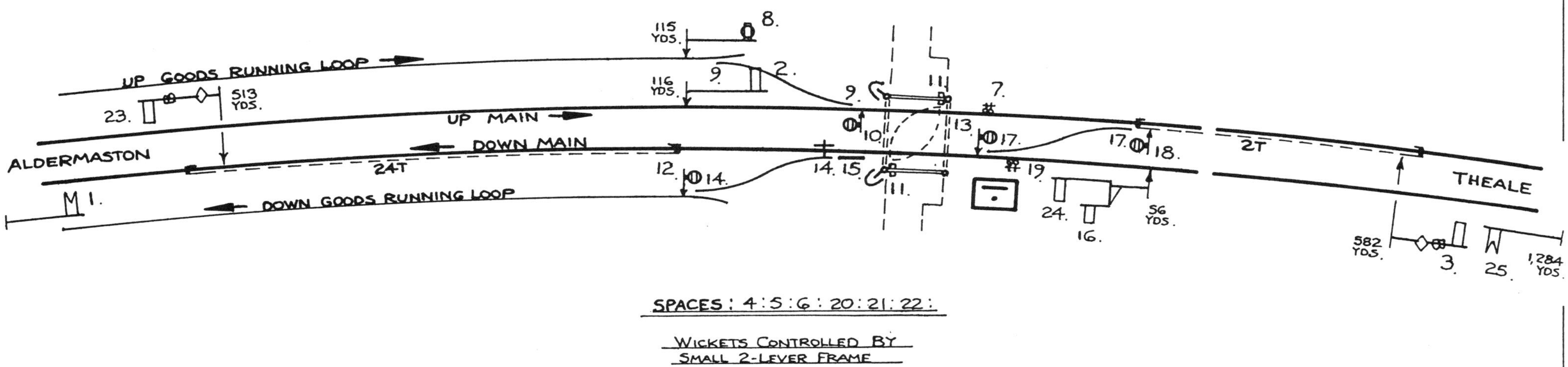

GWR TYPE 13 SIGNAL BOX, 24' 2" X 11' 2" ELEV. 8'.
OPENED 14-02-1943 TO REPLACE EARLIER BOX.
VT 5-BAR FRAME, 4" CENTRES.
FPL STANDS NORMALLY "OUT".
SPAGNOLETTI BLOCK ON MAIN LINES, LATER WR 3-POSITION.
PERMISSIVE BLOCK TO ALDERMASTON ON GOODS LINES.
CLOSING SWITCH:- ONE (ADDED).
GATES WORKED BY WHEEL.

31-03-1963: Up Goods Running Loop taken out of use. Levers 8, 9, & 10 made spare.

BOX CLOSED 05-12-1977. AREA THEN CONTROLLED BY READING PANEL.

THEALE

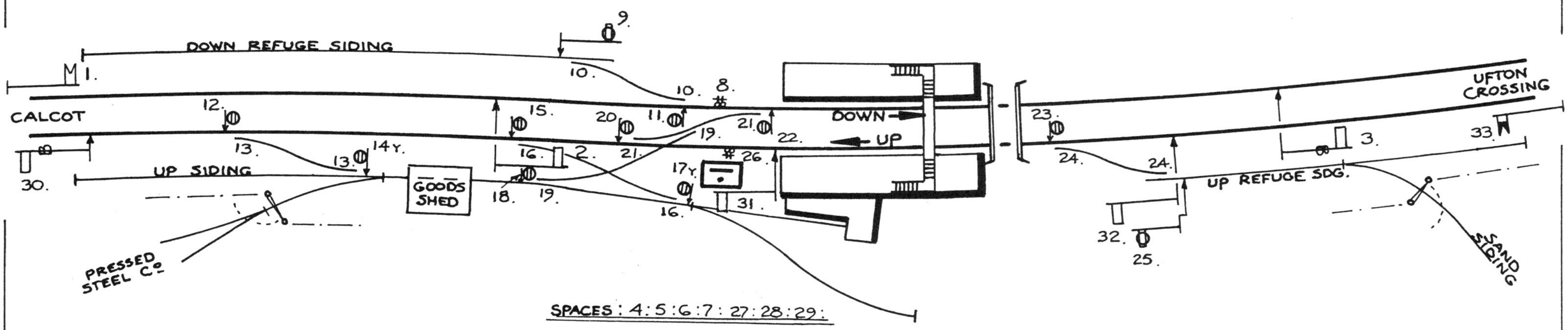

GWR TYPE 7D SIGNAL BOX, 25' X 11' ELEVATED 8'.
OPENED 1920 TO REPLACE ORIGINAL.
VT 3-BAR FRAME, 4" CENTRES.
SPAGNOLETTI BLOCK, LATER WR 3-POSITION.
CLOSING SWITCH:- ONE (REMOVED 1965).

13-08-1961: Slip Points 19 and Disc 18 abolished.

Feb. 1972: Down Refuge Siding taken out of use, together with connection between Up Main and Up Siding adjacent to signal box. Levers 9, 10, 11,15, 16, and 17 made spare.

23-02-1975: Points 13 and Discs 12 & 14 taken out of use.

BOX CLOSED 19-09-1977. AREA THEN CONTROLLED BY READING PANEL.

CALCOT

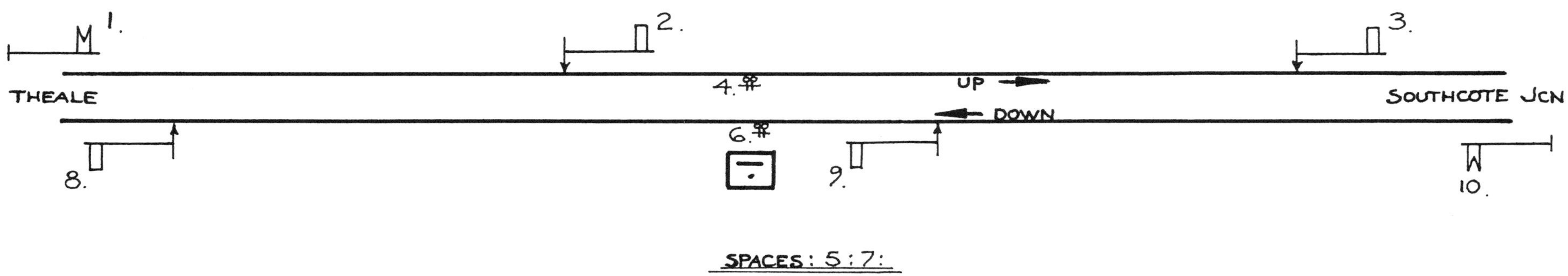

GWR BOX, TYPE UNCERTAIN.
OPENED 1905.
STUD LOCKING FRAME, 5¼" CENTRES.
SPAGNOLETTI BLOCK.
CLOSING SWITCH:- ONE.

BOX CLOSED 17-11-1963

SOUTHCOTE JCN. (1950)

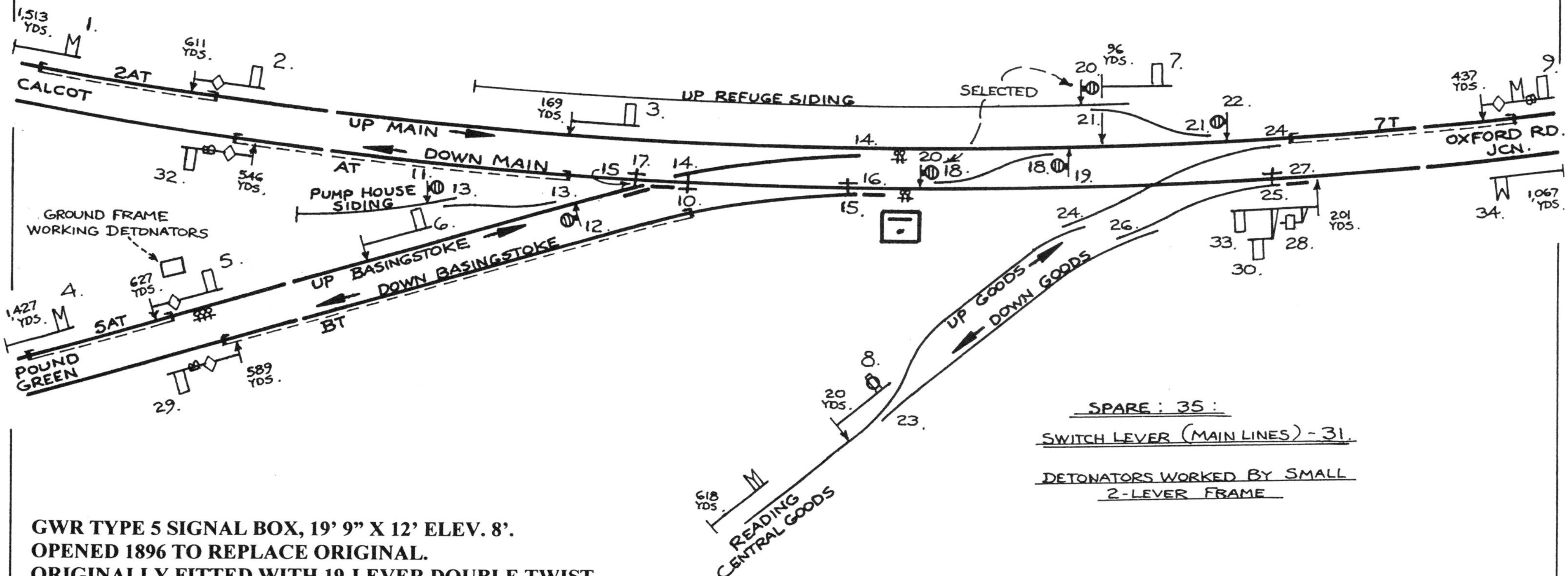

SPARE : 35 :

SWITCH LEVER (MAIN LINES) - 31.

DETONATORS WORKED BY SMALL 2-LEVER FRAME

GWR TYPE 5 SIGNAL BOX, 19' 9" X 12' ELEV. 8'.
OPENED 1896 TO REPLACE ORIGINAL.
ORIGINALLY FITTED WITH 19-LEVER DOUBLE TWIST FRAME. STUD LOCKING FRAME, 5¼" CENTRES, OF 35 LEVERS INSTALLED 1906 AND CONVERTED TO VT 5-BAR LOCKING 1956.
FPLs STAND NORMALLY "OUT".
SPAGNOLETTI BLOCK ON MAIN AND BASINGSTOKE LINES.
WOODEN TRAIN STAFF TO READING CENTRAL GDS.
CLOSING SWITCH:- ONE (ON MAIN LINES).

26-05-1956: **Junction to Reading Central Goods Line simplified. Points 23 & 24 abolished. Crossover 18 removed and new crossover 24 provided Oxford Road Junction side of 25 Points.**

01-09-1963: **Up Refuge Siding abolished.**

BOX CLOSED 25-04-1965. AREA THEN CONTROLLED BY READING PANEL.

OXFORD ROAD JC.

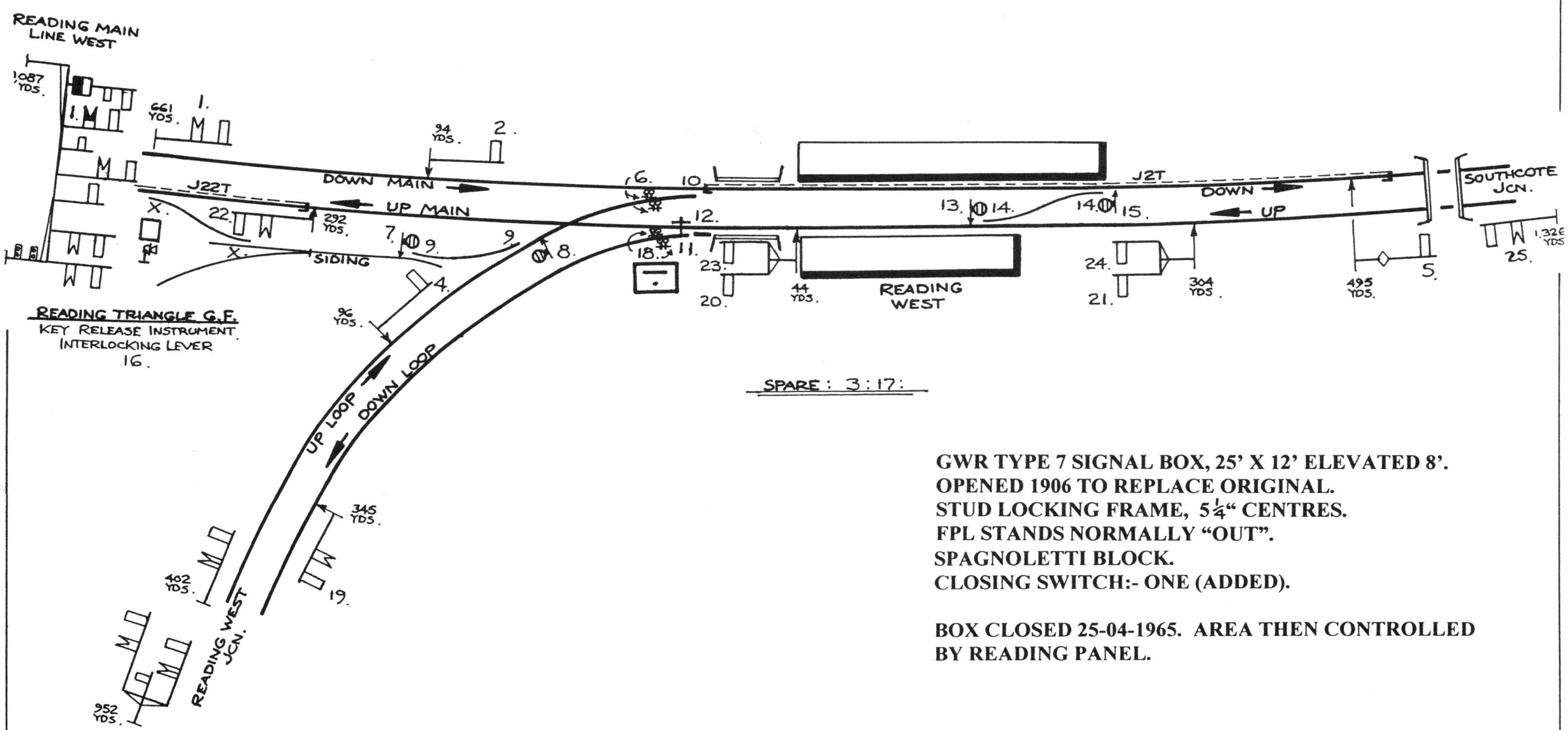

SPARE: 3: 17:

GWR TYPE 7 SIGNAL BOX, 25’ X 12’ ELEVATED 8’.
OPENED 1906 TO REPLACE ORIGINAL.
STUD LOCKING FRAME, 5¼“ CENTRES.
FPL STANDS NORMALLY “OUT”.
SPAGNOLETTI BLOCK.
CLOSING SWITCH:- ONE (ADDED).

BOX CLOSED 25-04-1965. AREA THEN CONTROLLED BY READING PANEL.

SECTION TWO

BERKS & HANTS BASINGSTOKE BRANCH

LINE OPENED 01-11-1848.

BASINGSTOKE (GWR)

"BASINGSTOKE 'C'" FROM 27-05-1954

GWR BRICK SIGNAL BOX,
OPENED 1892.
DOUBLE TWIST FRAME, 5¼" CENTRES.
FPLs STAND NORMALLY OUT.
SPAGNOLETTI BLOCK TO SHERFIELD.
PREECE 3-WIRE BLOCK TO BASINGSTOKE 'A'
UNTIL 1954, THEN SR 3-POSITION OPEN.
ILLUMINATED DIAGRAM PROVIDED 1954.
CLOSING SWITCH:- NIL.

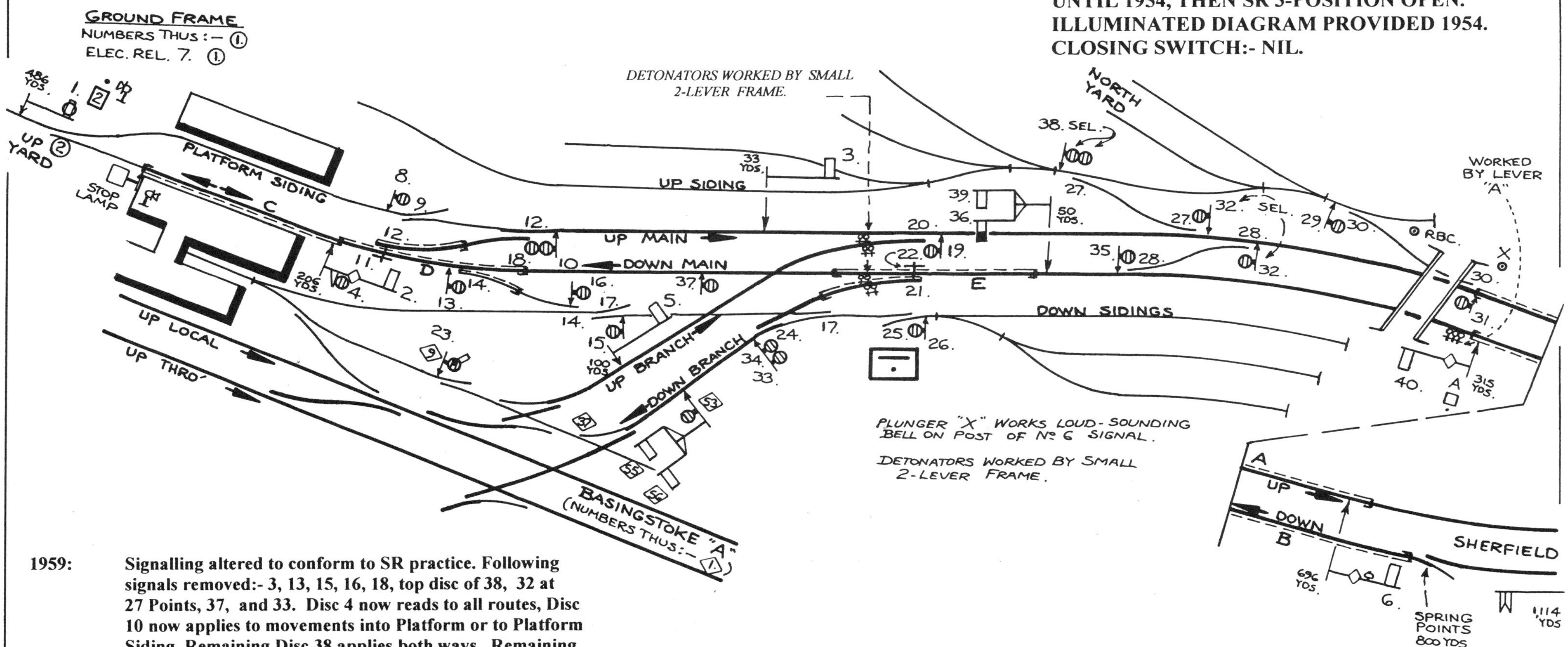

1959:	**Signalling altered to conform to SR practice. Following signals removed:- 3, 13, 15, 16, 18, top disc of 38, 32 at 27 Points, 37, and 33. Disc 4 now reads to all routes, Disc 10 now applies to movements into Platform or to Platform Siding, Remaining Disc 38 applies both ways. Remaining Disc 32 applies to Sidings, straight back on Up Main, or through Crossover 28. Disc 34 now applies both ways.**

26-03-1965: Points 27 abolished and Disc 38 removed.

08-05-1965: Down Sidings abolished. Points 14, 17, 25, and Disc 26 taken out of use.

BOX CLOSED 19-11-1966. AREA THEN CONTROLLED FROM NEW "BASINGSTOKE" PANEL BOX.

SHERFIELD

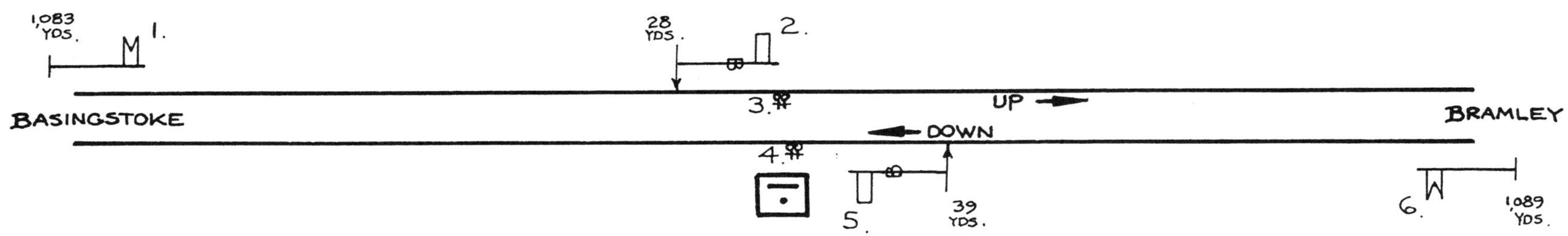

GWR TYPE 28 SIGNAL BOX, 12' X 11' ELEVATED 8'.
OPENED 09-05-1940.
TYPE OF FRAME NOT RECORDED.
SPAGNOLETTI BLOCK.
CLOSING SWITCH:- ONE.

DATE OF CLOSURE UNCERTAIN. GONE BY OCT. 1946.

BRAMLEY SOUTH

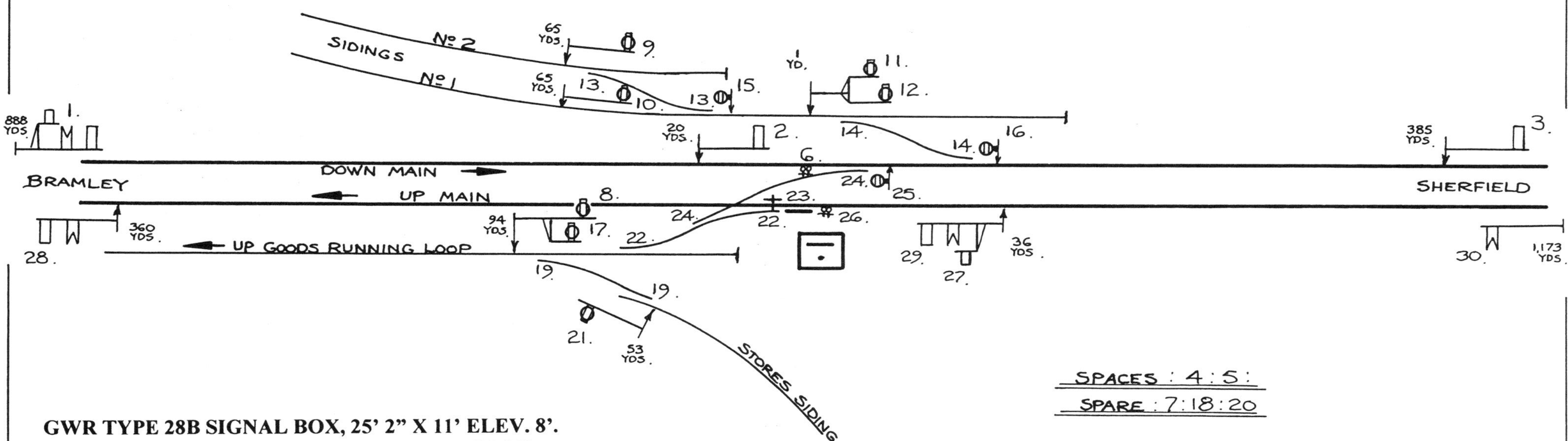

SPACES : 4 : 5 :
SPARE : 7 : 18 : 20

GWR TYPE 28B SIGNAL BOX, 25' 2" X 11' ELEV. 8'.
OPENED 1917 FOR NEW GOVERNMENT DEPOT.
STUD LOCKING FRAME, 5¼" CENTRES.
FPL STANDS NORMALLY "OUT".
SPAGNOLETTI BLOCK ON MAIN LINES.
PERMISSIVE BLOCK TO BRAMLEY ON UP GOODS.
CLOSING SWITCH:- ONE.

BOX CLOSED c. 1924 AND REPLACED BY GROUND FRAME – SEE NEXT PAGE.

BRAMLEY (1925)

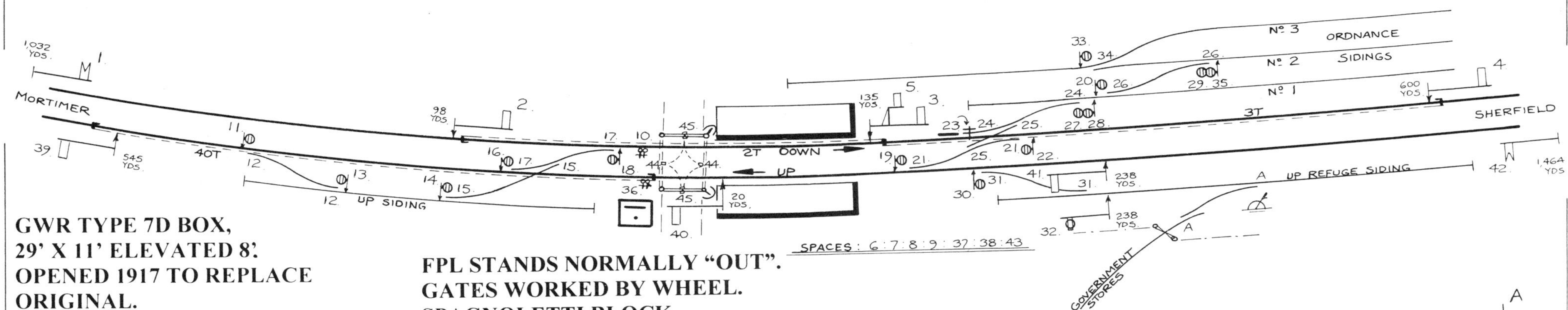

GWR TYPE 7D BOX,
29' X 11' ELEVATED 8'.
OPENED 1917 TO REPLACE ORIGINAL.
VT 3-BAR FRAME, 4" CENTRES.

FPL STANDS NORMALLY "OUT".
GATES WORKED BY WHEEL.
SPAGNOLETTI BLOCK.
CLOSING SWITCH:- NIL.

SEE BELOW FOR ARRANGEMENT AFTER CLOSURE OF SOUTH BOX.

(1944)

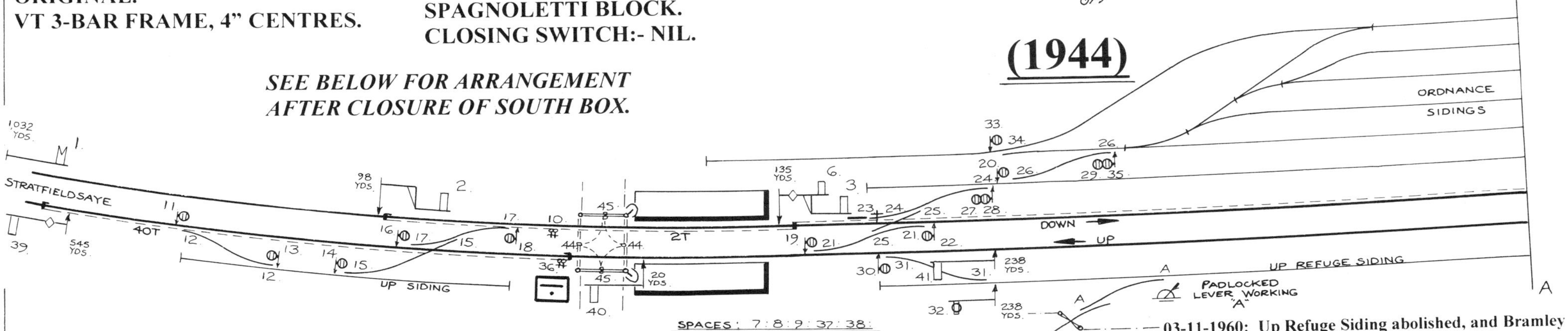

✱ DOWN LINE INSTRUMENT RELEASES INTERLOCKING LEVER ⑦
UP LINE INSTRUMENT RELEASES INTERLOCKING LEVER ⑧

DETAILS OF BOX AND EQUIPMENT AS IN UPPER DIAGRAM.

03-11-1960: Up Refuge Siding abolished, and Bramley South G.F. replaced by new 3-lever frame on Down side of line.

30-12-1963: Up Siding abolished. Levers 11, 12, 13, 14 & 15 made spare.

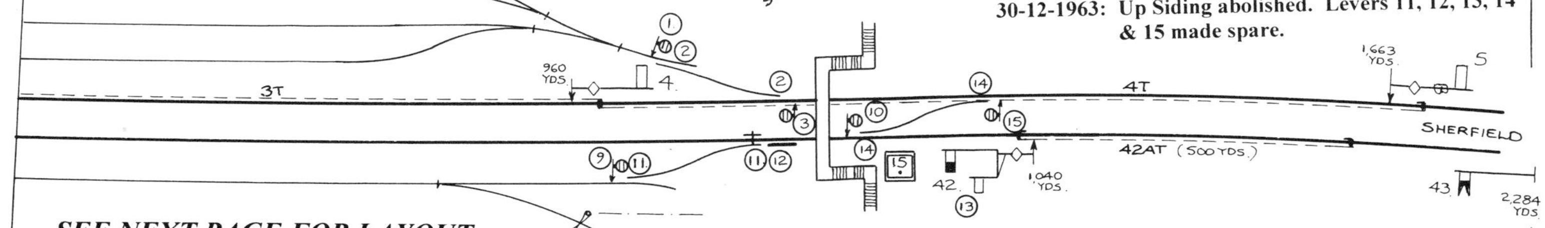

SEE NEXT PAGE FOR LAYOUT AFTER 1966.

BRAMLEY GROUND FRAME

NUMBERS THUS:- ①
ELCTRICALLY RELEASED FROM SIGNAL BOX BY KEY RELEASE INSTRUMENTS. ✱

BRAMLEY (1967)

THIS ARRANGEMENT FULLY OPERATIVE FROM 1966. TCB TO READING FROM 24-04-1965 AND TO BASINGSTOKE FROM 20-11-1966.

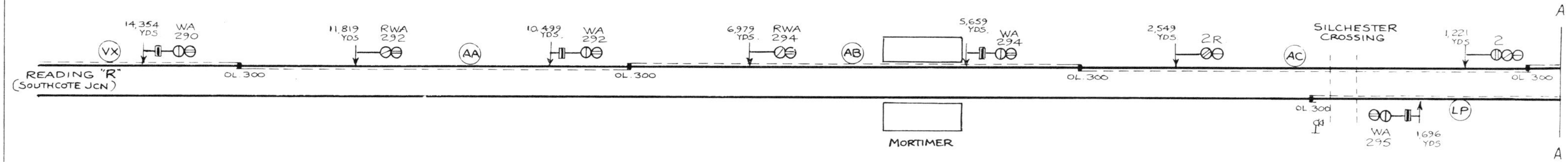

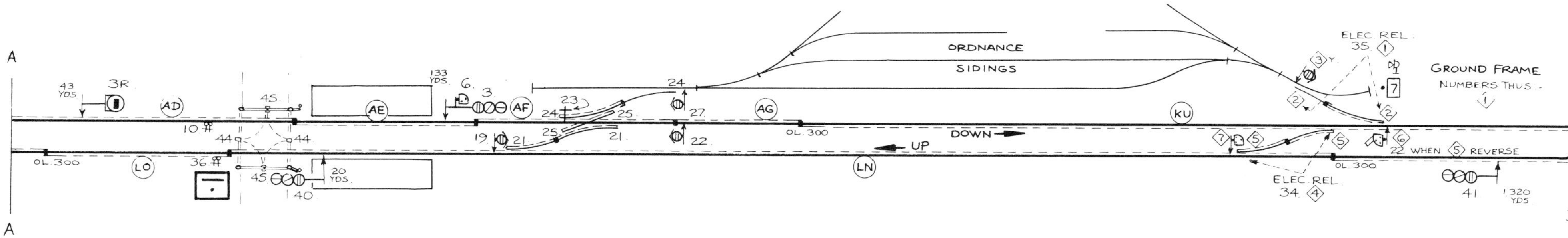

SPARE : 1 : 4 : 5 : 11 : 12 : 13 : 14 : 15 : 16 : 17 : 18 : 20 : 26 : 28 : 29 : 30 : 31 : 32 : 33 : 39 : 42 : 43 :

SPACES : 7 : 8 : 9 : 37 : 38

DETAILS OF BOX AND LEVER FRAME AS ON PREVIOUS PAGE. TRACK CIRCUIT BLOCK TO READING AND BASINGSTOKE WITH DIGITAL TRAIN DESCRIBERS AND EMERGENCY BLOCK BELLS, ILLUMINATED DIAGRAM.

09-03-1971: **Facing connection No. 24 from Down Main to Sidings and crossover taken out of use. Levers 19, 21, 22, 23, 24, 25, 27 made spare.**

23-10-1977: **Box downgraded to Ground Frame controlling crossing only. Release of Sidings & Crossover transferred to Basingstoke.**

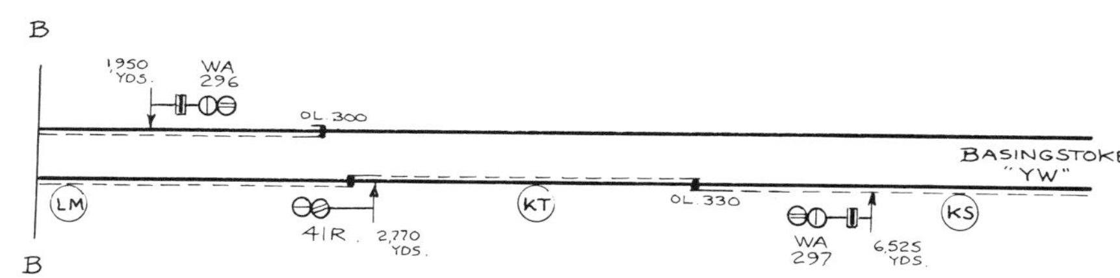

BOX CLOSED 25-10-1977. LEVEL CROSSING THEN AHBs.

STRATFIELD (1918)

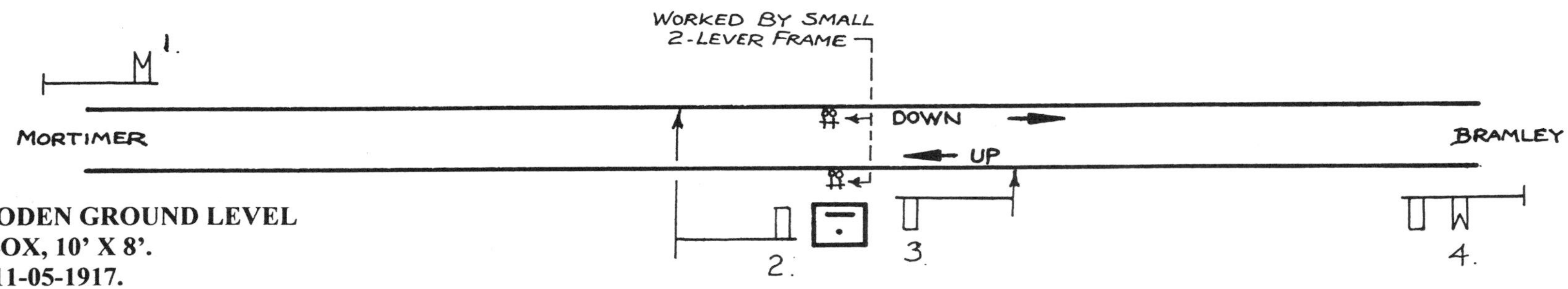

GWR WOODEN GROUND LEVEL
SIGNAL BOX, 10' X 8'.
OPENED 11-05-1917.
NO INFORMATION ON LOCKING FRAME.
SPAGNOLETTI BLOCK.
CLOSING SWITCH:- ONE.

BOX CLOSED 1924. REPLACED DURING WORLD WAR 2 BY "STRATFIELDSAYE" - SEE BELOW. STRUCTURE WENT TO COTFIELD (Near Exeter).

STRATFIELDSAYE (1941)

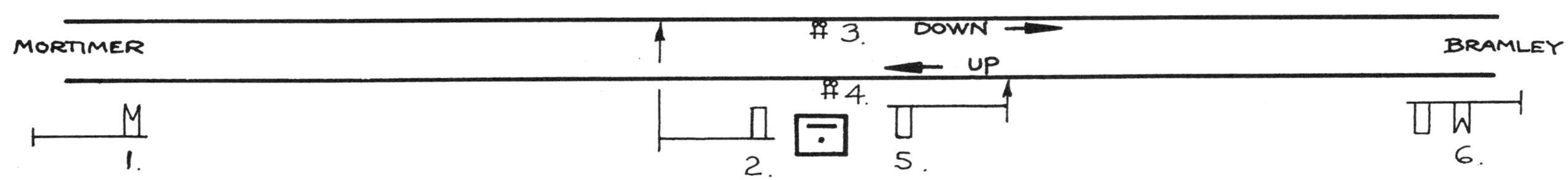

WOODEN GROUND LEVEL BOX,
OPENED 03-01-1940 ON SITE 8 CHAINS NORTH
OF FORMER "STRATFIELD" BOX.
TYPE OF FRAME NOT RECORDED.
SPAGNOLETTI BLOCK.
CLOSING SWITCH:- ONE.

BOX CLOSED 03-09-1950

MORTIMER

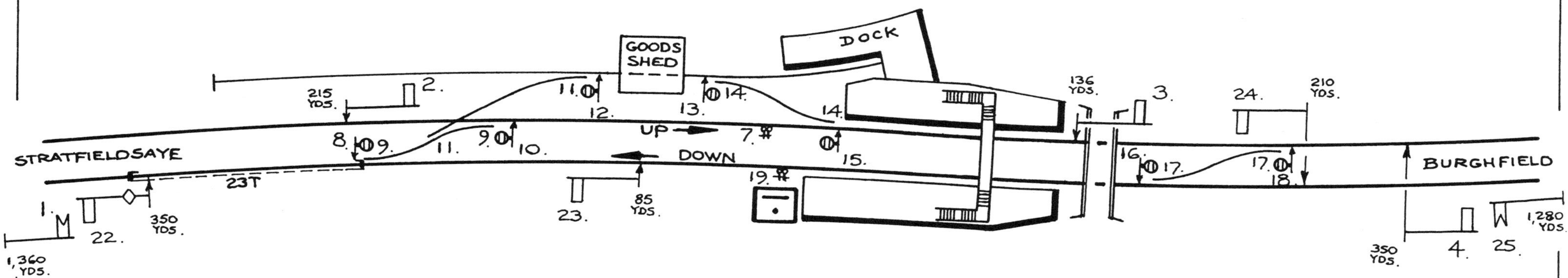

SPACES: 5 : 6 : 20 : 21 :

GWR TYPE 3 SIGNAL BOX,
OPENED 1889.
TYPE OF FRAME NOT RECORDED.
SPAGNOLETTI BLOCK.
CLOSING SWITCH:- ONE.

17-06-1963: **All Points and Discs taken out of use.**

BOX CLOSED 28-06-1964

BURGHFIELD

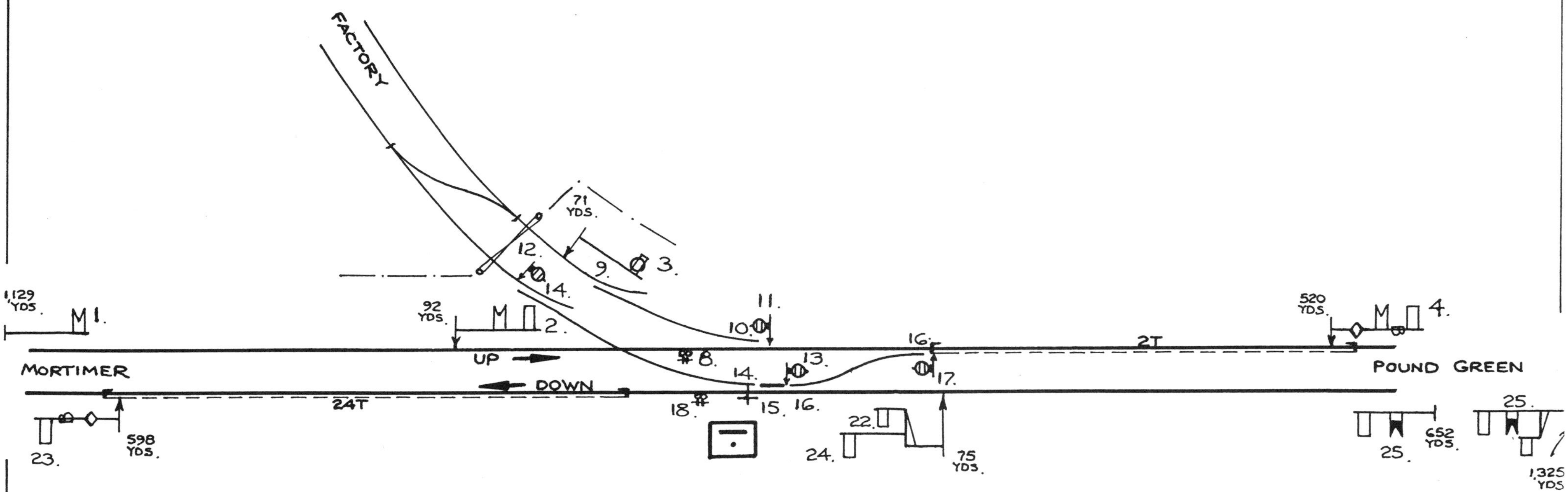

SPACES: 5:6:7:19:20:21:

GWR BOX, TYPE UNCERTAIN, 22' X 12' ELEVATED 8'
OPENED 22-06-1941 FOR NEW GOVERNMENT FACTORY
TYPE OF FRAME UNCOMFIRMED.
FPL STANDS NORMALLY "OUT".
SPAGNOLETTI BLOCK ON MAIN LINES.
TELEPHONE WORKING TO FACTORY.
CLOSING SWITCH:- ONE

BOX CLOSED 11-05-1958 AND ALL CONNECTIONS
TAKEN OUT OF USE.

POUND GREEN

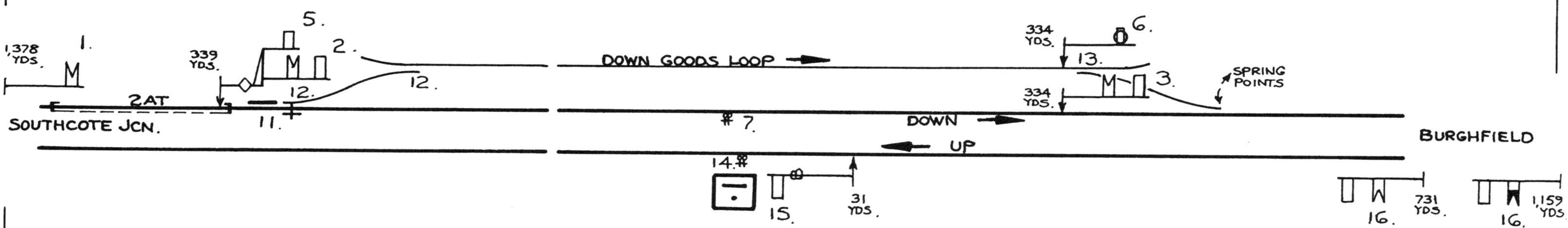

SPACES: 4:8:9:10:

GWR BOX, TYPE UNCERTAIN, 15' X 11' ELEVATED 8'.
OPENED 16-02-1940.
TYPE OF FRAME NOT RECORDED.
SPAGNOLETTI BLOCK.
CLOSING SWITCH:- ONE

BOX CLOSED AND LOOP ABOLISHED 27-02-1950

SECTION THREE

DIDCOT, NEWBURY AND SOUTHAMPTON RAILWAY

(ABSORBED BY GWR 1923)

LINE OPENED: DIDCOT TO NEWBURY 12-04-1882.
NEWBURY TO WINCHESTER 04-05-1885.
WINCHESTER TO SHAWFORD 04-09-1891.

CLOSED TO PASSENGERS: SHAWFORD TO NEWBURY 07-03-1960.
DIDCOT TO NEWBURY 10-09-1962.

CLOSED COMPLETELY FROM WINCHESTER TO DIDCOT 09-08-1964.

SHAWFORD JUNCTION TO WINCHESTER CLOSED COMPLETELY 04-04-1966.

WINCHESTER (1923)

"WINCHESTER CHESIL" FROM c.1954.

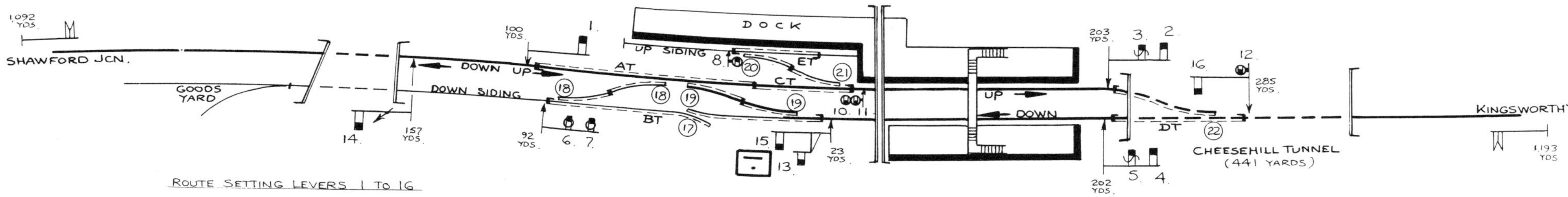

ROUTE SETTING LEVERS 1 TO 16

INDIVIDUAL POINT SLIDES (17) TO (22) RELEASED BY INTERLOCKING LEVER - 9.

ROUTE-SETTING FRAME REPLACED BY CONVENTIONAL FRAME JUNE 1933 – SEE LOWER DIAGRAM.

GWR TYPE 8 SIGNAL BOX, 17' X 10' ELEVATED 7' AND EXTENDED 1942.
OPENED 1922 TO REPLACE ORIGINAL.
SIEMENS' EXPERIMENTAL ROUTE SETTING FRAME.

TYER'S No. 6 TABLET TO SHAWFORD JUNCTION.
CLOSING SWITCH:- NIL.
ELECTRIC KEY TOKEN TO KINGSWORTHY.

THIS LAYOUT OPERATIVE FROM 14-10-1942, WHEN LOOP EXTENDED THROUGH TUNNEL.

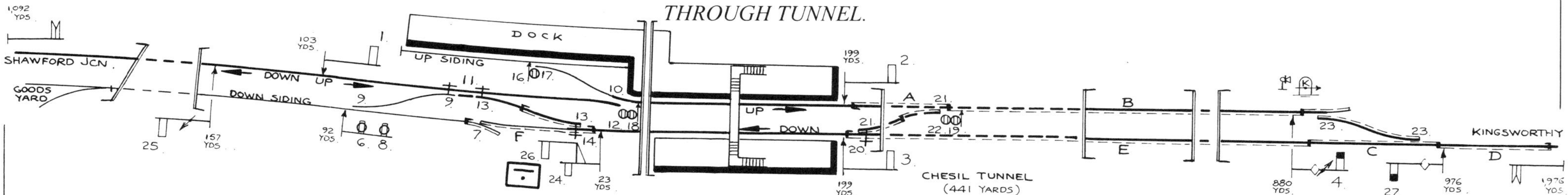

SPACES: 5 : 15:

DESCRIPTION OF BOX STRUCTURE AND INSTRUMENTS AS FOR UPPER DIAGRAM.
VT 5-BAR FRAME INSTALLED JUNE 1933 TO REPLACE EXPERIMENTAL SIEMANS' EQUIPMENT.

FPLs STAND NORMALLY "OUT" EXCEPT 11 ON 13, WHICH STANDS NORMALLY "IN".
POINTS 23 WORKED BY MOTOR (HAND GENERATOR)

SR TYPE ILLUMINATED DIAGRAM.

BOX CLOSED 04-04-1966 (LINE CLOSED)

KINGSWORTHY (1920)

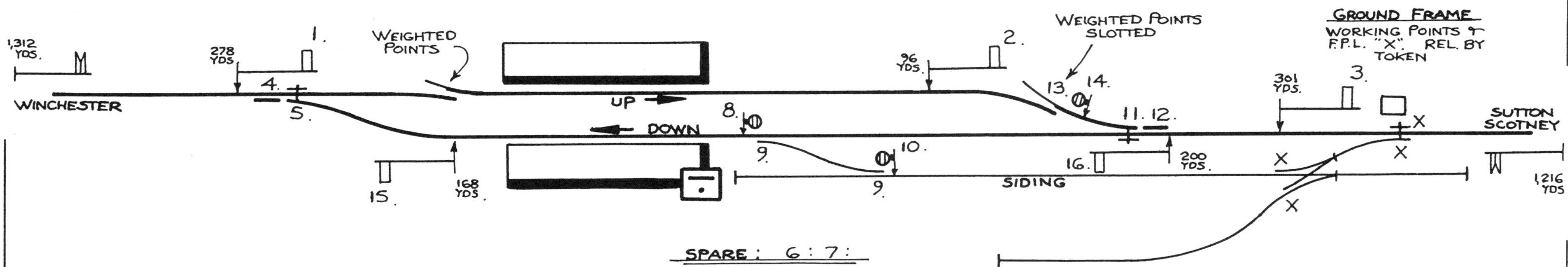

GWR TYPE 27C SIGNAL BOX, 21' X 12' ELEVATED 8'.
OPENED 1909 (ADDITIONAL CROSSING PLACE).
TYPE OF FRAME NOT RECORDED.
FPLs STAND NORMALLY "OUT".
ELECTRIC TRAIN STAFF UNTIL 1911, THEN ELECTRIC KEY TOKEN.
CLOSING SWITCH:- NIL.

BOX MOVED TO NEW POSITION AND FITTED WITH LARGER FRAME 21-12-1942 – SEE NEXT PAGE.

KINGSWORTHY (1943)

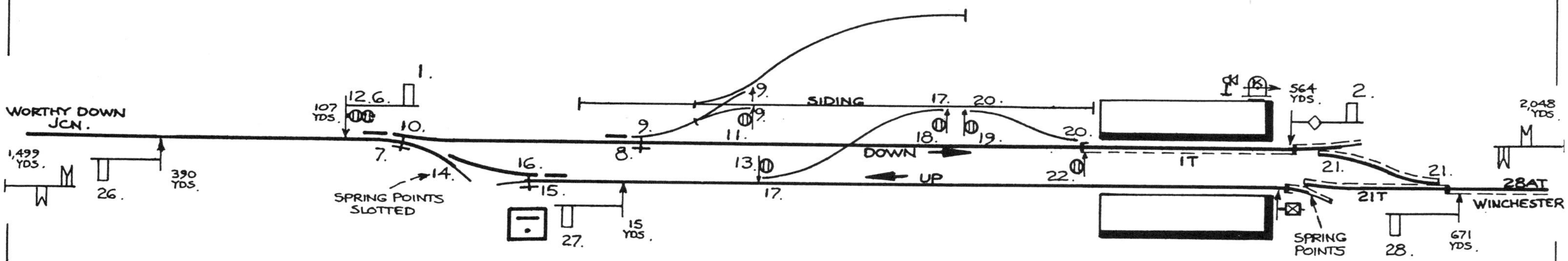

SPACES : 3 : 4 : 5 : 23 : 24 : 25 :

GWR TYPE 27C SIGNAL BOX MOVED FROM FORMER LOCATION (SEE PREVIOUS PAGE) 21-12-1942.
VT 5-BAR FRAME, 4" CENTRES.
FPLs STAND NORMALLY "OUT".
POINTS 21 WORKED BY MOTOR (HAND GENERATOR).
ELECTRIC KEY TOKEN.
CLOSING SWITCH:- NIL.

BOX CLOSED 30-01-1955 AND LOOP ABOLISHED, ALL TRAFFIC TO PASS OVER FORMER DOWN LOOP. TWO GROUND FRMAES PROVIDED TO WORK CONNECTIONS TO SIDINGS (FORMERLY 9 & 20).

WORTHY DOWN JCN.

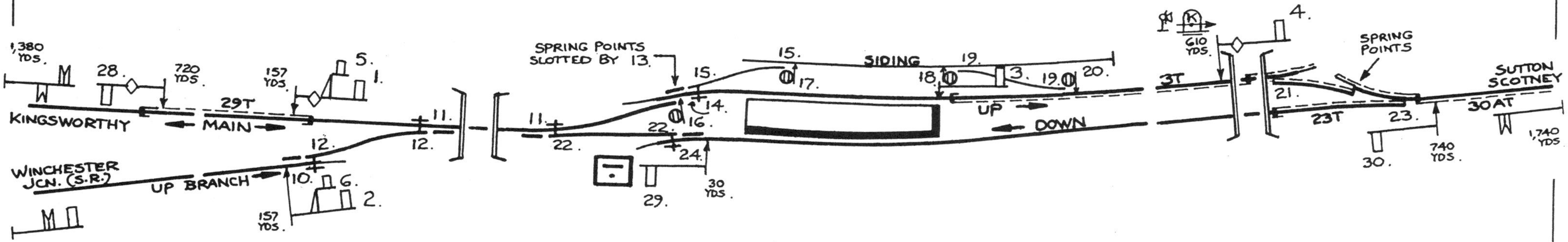

SPACES: 7:8:9:25:26:27:

GWR TYPE 13 SIGNAL BOX, 24' 2" X 12' ELEVATED 8'.
OPENED 14-02-1943. NEW LOOP AND JUNCTION.
VT 5-BAR FRAME, 4" CENTRES.
FPLs STAND NORMALLY "OUT".
POINTS 21 & 23 WORKED BY MOTOR (HAND GENERATOR).
ELECTRIC KEY TOKEN TO KINSWORTHY AND SUTTON SCOTNEY.
SPAGNOLETTI SINGLE PEGGING INSTRUMENT FROM WINCHESTER JUNCTION (SR).
CLOSING SWITCH:- NIL.

25-11-1951: Line from Winchester Junction abolished as through line but retained for wagon storage. Block instrument recovered. Points 12 and FPLs 10 & 11b disconnected from signal box, and will be worked on the ground as required. Arms and Lamps of Signals 2 & 6 removed.

24-02-1957: Siding taken out of use. Levers 5, 15, 16, 17, 18, 19, & 20 made spare.

BOX CLOSED 10-08-1964 (LINE CLOSED).

SUTTON SCOTNEY (1925)

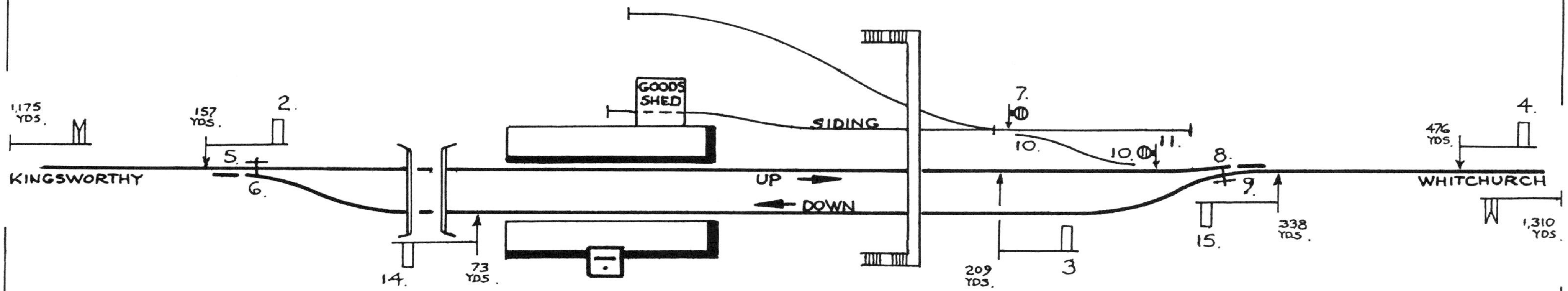

SPACES: 12: 13: 16:

SPARE: 1:

SAXBY & FARMER TIMBER SIGNAL BOX,
OPENED 04-05-1885.
DETAILS OF LEVER FRAME UNKNOWN.
FPLs STAND NORMALLY "OUT".
TRAIN STAFF & TICKET UNTIL 1901, THEN ELECTRIC TRAIN STAFF UNTIL 1911, THEREAFTER ELECTRIC KEY TOKEN.
CLOSING SWITCH;- NIL.

BOX CLOSED 06-11-1942 – SEE NEXT PAGE FOR REPLACEMENT.

SUTTON SCOTNEY (1943)

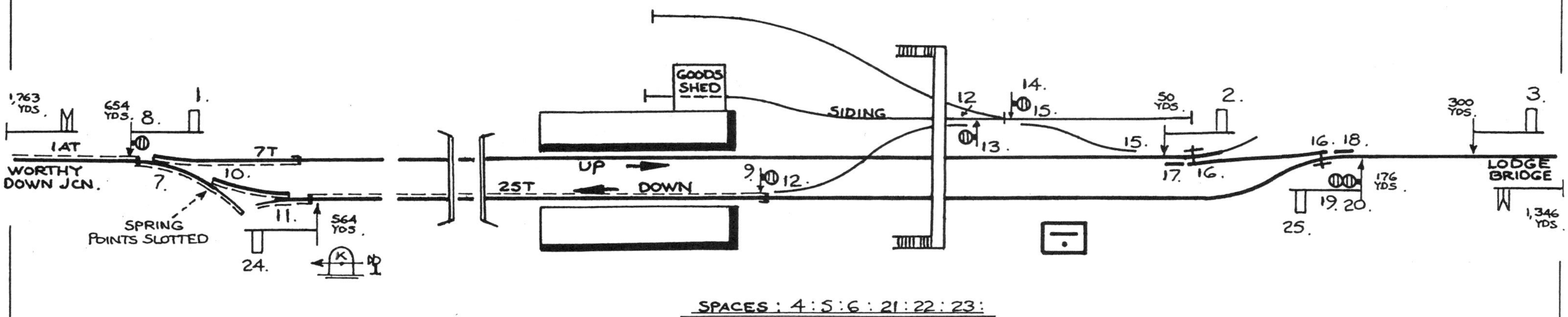

GWR TYPE 13 SIGNAL BOX, 24' 2" X 12' ELEVATED 8'.
OPENED 06-11-1942 AS REPLACEMENT FOR BOX ON PREVIOUS PAGE (EXTENDED LOOP FOR WAR TRAFFIC)
VT 5-BAR FRAME, 4" CENTRES.
FPLs STAND NORMALLY "OUT".
POINTS 7, 10 & 11 WORKED BY MOTOR (HAND GENERATOR).
ELECTRIC KEY TOKEN.
CLOSING SWITCH:- NIL

BOX CLOSED 10-08-1964 (LINE CLOSED).

LODGE BRIDGE

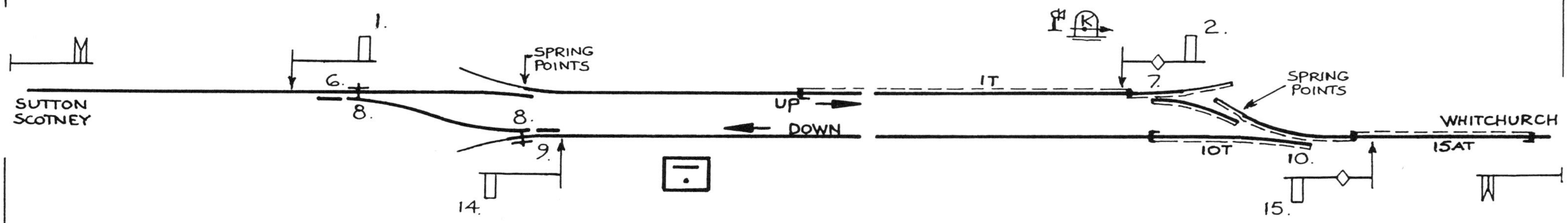

GWR TYPE 13 SIGNAL BOX, 24’ 2” X 12’ ELEVATED 8’.
OPENED 28-03-1943 AS ADDITIONAL CROSSING LOOP FOR WAR TRAFFIC.
VT 5-BAR FRAME, 4” CENTRES.
FPLs STAND NORMALLY “OUT”.
POINTS 10 WORKED BY MOTOR (HAND GENERATOR).
ELECTRIC KEY TOKEN.
CLOSING SWITCH:- NIL.

BOX CLOSED AND LOOP ABOLISHED 07-03-1950.

WHITCHURCH (HANTS) (1920)

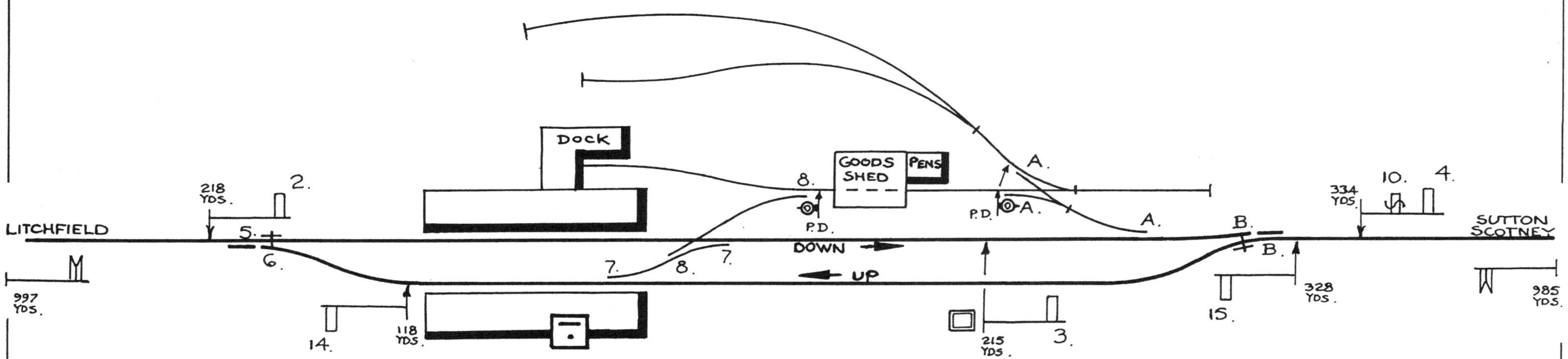

WHITCHURCH GROUND FRAME
WORKING POINTS & FPL "A" AND "B".

ELECTRICALLY RELEASED FROM SIGNAL BOX.
INTERLOCKING LEVER FOR POINTS "A" - 9.
INTERLOCKING LEVER FOR POINTS "B" - 12.
INTERLOCKING LEVER FOR FPL "B" - 11

SAXBY & FARMER TIMBER SIGNAL BOX.
OPENED 1897.
DETAILS OF LEVER FRAME UNKNOWN.
FPLs STAND NORMALLY "OUT".
TRAIN STAFF & TICKET UNTIL 1901, THEN ELECTRIC TRAIN STAFF, THEREAFTER ELECTRIC KEY TOKEN.
CLOSING SWITCH:- NIL.

BOX CLOSED 03-03-1943 – SEE NEXT PAGE FOR REPLACEMENT.

WHITCHURCH (HANTS) (1944)

"WHITCHURCH TOWN" FROM APRIL 1950

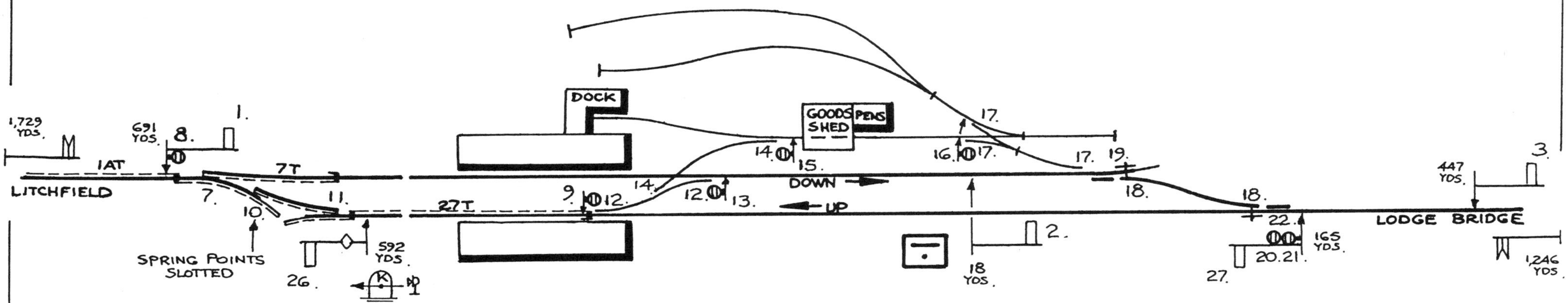

SPACES : 4 : 5 : 6 : 23 : 24 : 25 :

GWR TYPE 13 SIGNAL BOX, 24' 2" X 12' ELEVATED 8'.
OPENED 03-03-1943 TO REPLACE BOX ON PREVIOUS PAGE – EXTENDED LOOP FOR WAR TRAFFIC.
VT 5-BAR FRAME, 4" CENTRES.
FPLs STAND NORMALLY "OUT".
POINTS 7, 10 & 11 WORKED BY MOTOR (HAND GENERATOR)
ELECTRIC KEY TOKEN.
CLOSING SWITCH:- NIL.

06-06-1964:- Points 12, 14, 17, and Discs 8, 9, 13, 15, 16, 20 & 21 taken out of use.

BOX CLOSED 10-08-1964 (LINE CLOSED)

LITCHFIELD (1925)

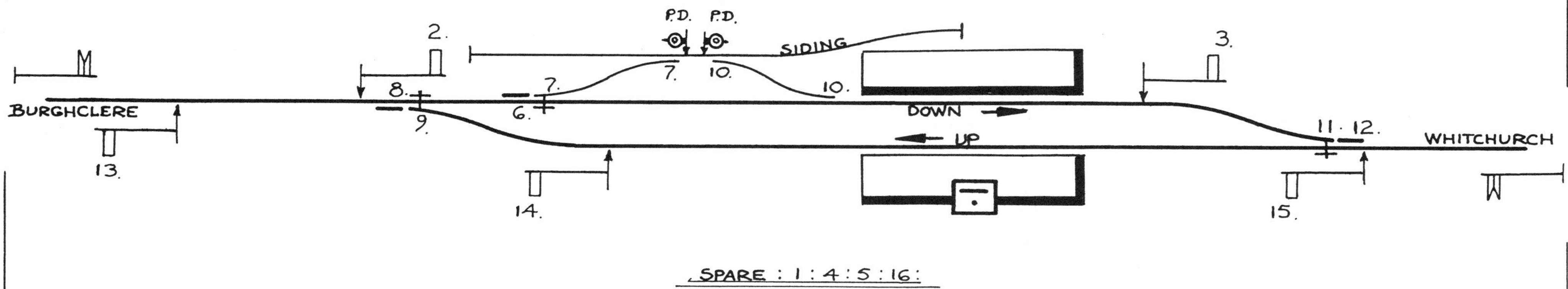

SAXBY & FARMER TIMBER SIGNAL BOX,
OPENED 04 –05-1885.
DETAILS OF LEVER FRAME UNKNOWN.
FPLs STAND NORMALLY "OUT".
TRAIN STAFF & TICKET UNTIL 1901, THEN ELECTRIC TRAIN STAFF, THEREAFTER ELECTRIC KEY TOKEN.
CLOSING SWITCH:- NIL.

BOX CLOSED 05-07-1936 AND LOOP ABOLISHED. GROUND FRAME PROVIDED TO CONTROL SIDING POINTS. LOOP LATER REINSTATED - SEE NEXT PAGE.

LITCHFIELD (1944)

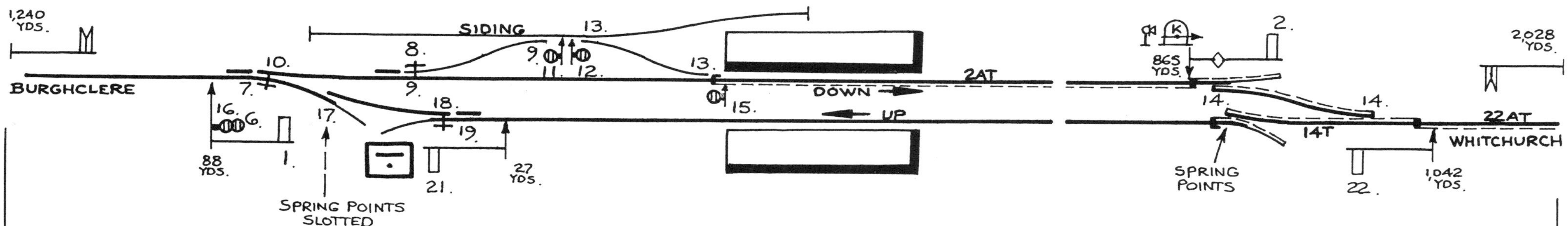

SPACES: 3: 4: 5: 20:

GWR TYPE 13 SIGNAL BOX, 24' 2" X 12' ELEVATED 8'.
OPENED 03-03-1943 FOR REINSTATEMENT OF LOOP.
VT 5-BAR FRAME, 4" CENTRES.
FPLs STAND NORMALLY "OUT".
POINTS 14 WORKED BY MOTOR (HAND GENERATOR).
ELECTRIC KEY TOKEN.
CLOSING SWITCH:- NIL.

BOX CLOSED 23-01-1955 AND LOOP ABOLISHED. ALL TRAFFIC TO PASS OVER FORMER DOWN LOOP.

BURGHCLERE (1925)

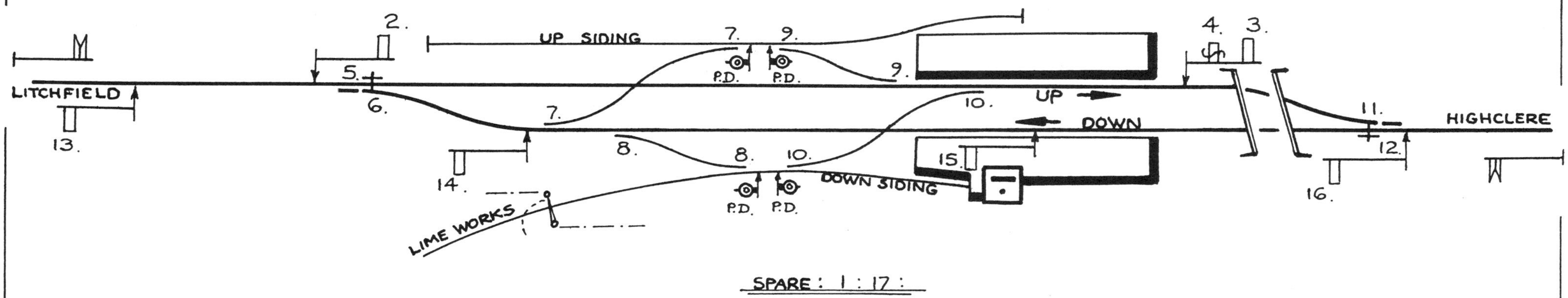

SAXBY & FARMER TIMBER SIGNAL BOX,
OPENED 04-05-1885.
TYPE OF LEVER FRAME UNKNOWN.
FPLs STAND NORMALLY "OUT".
TRAIN STAFF & TICKET UNTIL 1901, THEN ELECTRIC TRAIN STAFF, THEREAFTER ELECTRIC KEY TOKEN.
CLOSING SWITCH;- NIL.

BOX CLOSED 13-11-1942 - SEE NEXT PAGE FOR REPLACEMENT.

BURGHCLERE (1943)

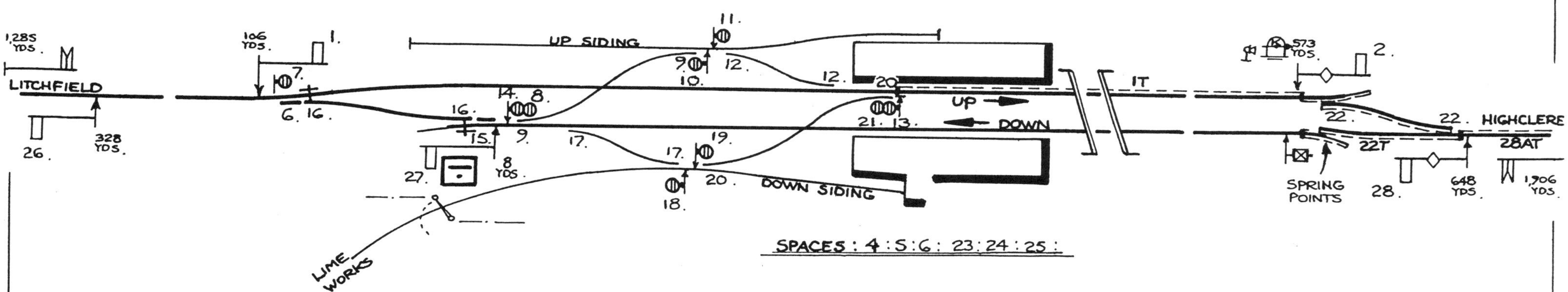

GWR TYPE 13 SIGNAL BOX, 24' 2" X 12' ELEVATED 8'.
OPENED 13-11-1942 TO REPLACE BOX SHOWN ON PREVIOUS PAGE – EXTENDED LOOP FOR WAR TRAFFIC.
VT 5-BAR FRAME, 4" CENTRES.
FPLs STAND NORMALLY "OUT".
POINTS 22 WORKED BY MOTOR (HAND GENERATOR).
ELECTRIC KEY TOKEN.
CLOSING SWITCH:- NIL.

22-01-1946: Down Siding taken out of use. Points 17, 20, and Discs 14, 18, 19, & 21 abolished.

08-06-1964: Up Siding taken out of use. Points 9, 12, and Discs 7, 8, 10, 11, & 13 abolished.

BOX CLOSED 10-08-1964 (LINE CLOSED).

HIGHCLERE (1925)

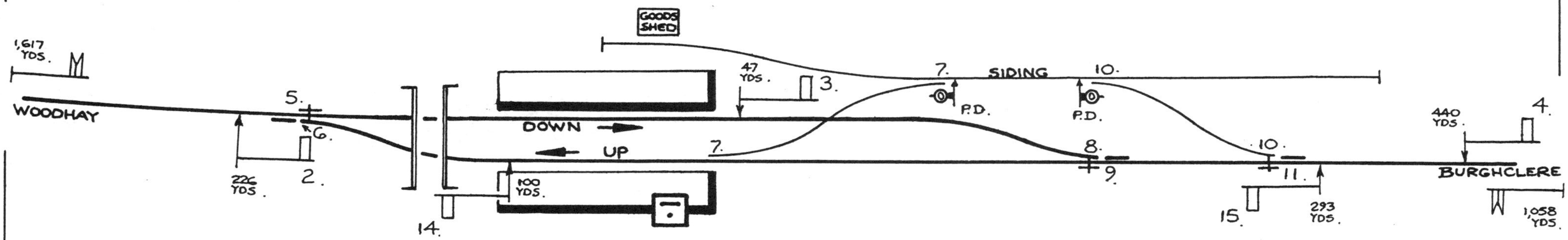

SPARE: 1:12:13:16:

SAXBY & FARMER TIMBER SIGNAL BOX,
OPENED 04-05-1885.
TYPE OF LEVER FRAME UNKNOWN.
FPLs STAND NORMALLY "OUT".
TRAIN STAFF & TICKET UNTIL 1901, THEN ELECTRIC TRAIN STAFF, THEREAFTER ELECTRIC KEY TOKEN.
CLOSING SWITCH:- NIL.

BOX CLOSED 28-10-1942 - SEE NEXT PAGE FOR REPLACEMENT.

HIGHCLERE (1943)

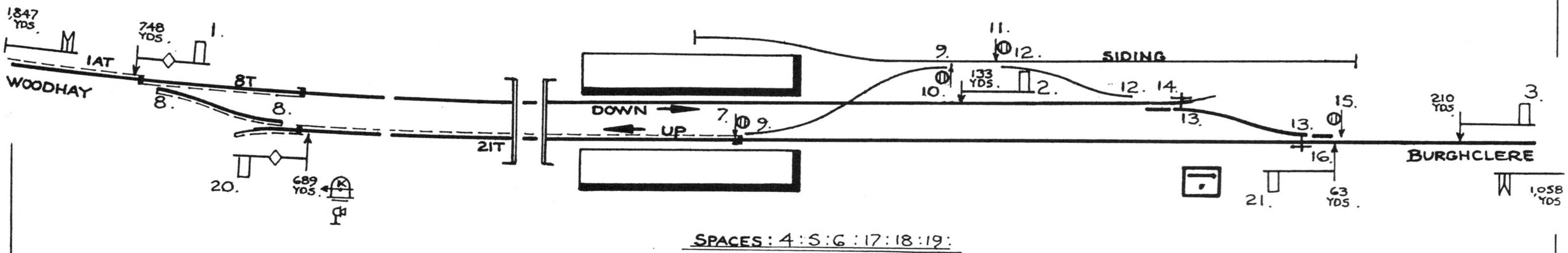

GWR TYPE 13 SIGNAL BOX, 24' 2" X 12' ELEVATED 8'.
OPENED 28-10-1942 AS REPLACEMENT FOR BOX ON PREVIOUS PAGE - EXTENDED LOOP FOR WAR TRAFFIC.
VT 5-BAR FRAME, 4" CENTRES.
FPLs STAND NORMALLY "OUT".
ELECTRIC KEY TOKEN.
CLOSING SWITCH:- NIL.

BOX CLOSED 06-02-1955 AND LOOP ABOLISHED.
GROUND FRAME PROVIDED TO WORK SIDING POINTS (FORMERLY No. 12).

WOODHAY (1920)

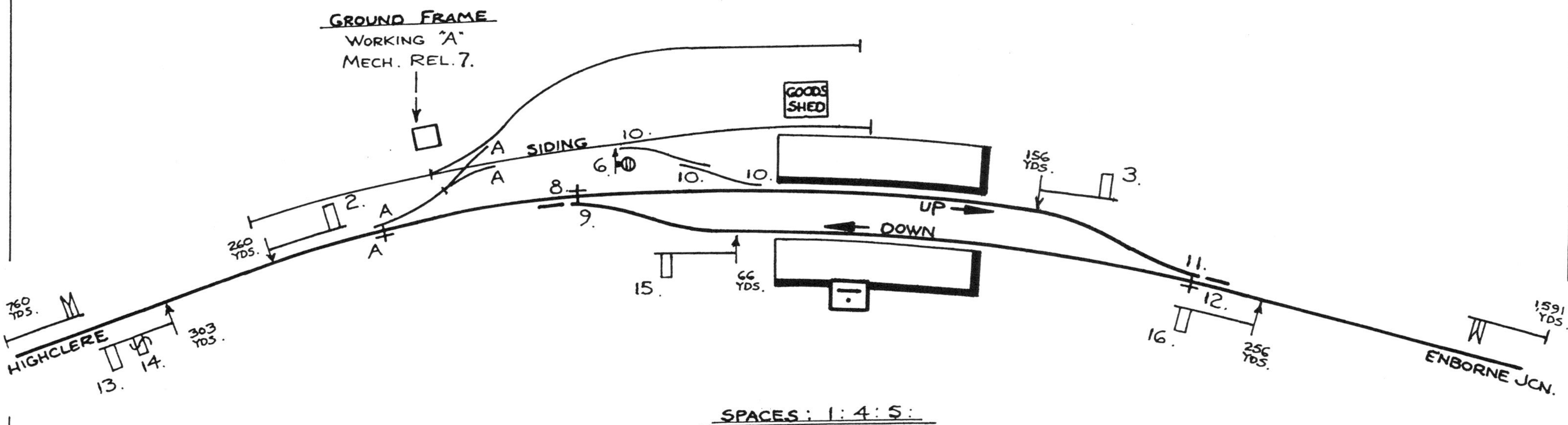

SAXBY & FARMER TIMBER SIGNAL BOX,
OPENED 04-05-1885.
TYPE OF LEVER FRAME UNKNOWN.
FPLs STAND NORMALLY "OUT".
TRAIN STAFF & TICKET UNTIL 1901, THEN ELECTRIC TRAIN STAFF, THEREAFTER ELECTRIC KEY TOKEN.
CLOSING SWITCH:- NIL.

BOX CLOSED 09-10-1942 - SEE NEXT PAGE FOR REPLACEMENT.

WOODHAY (1943)

SEE SECTION ONE OF THIS PUBLICATION FOR SIGNAL BOXES BETWEEN WOODHAY AND HERMITAGE.

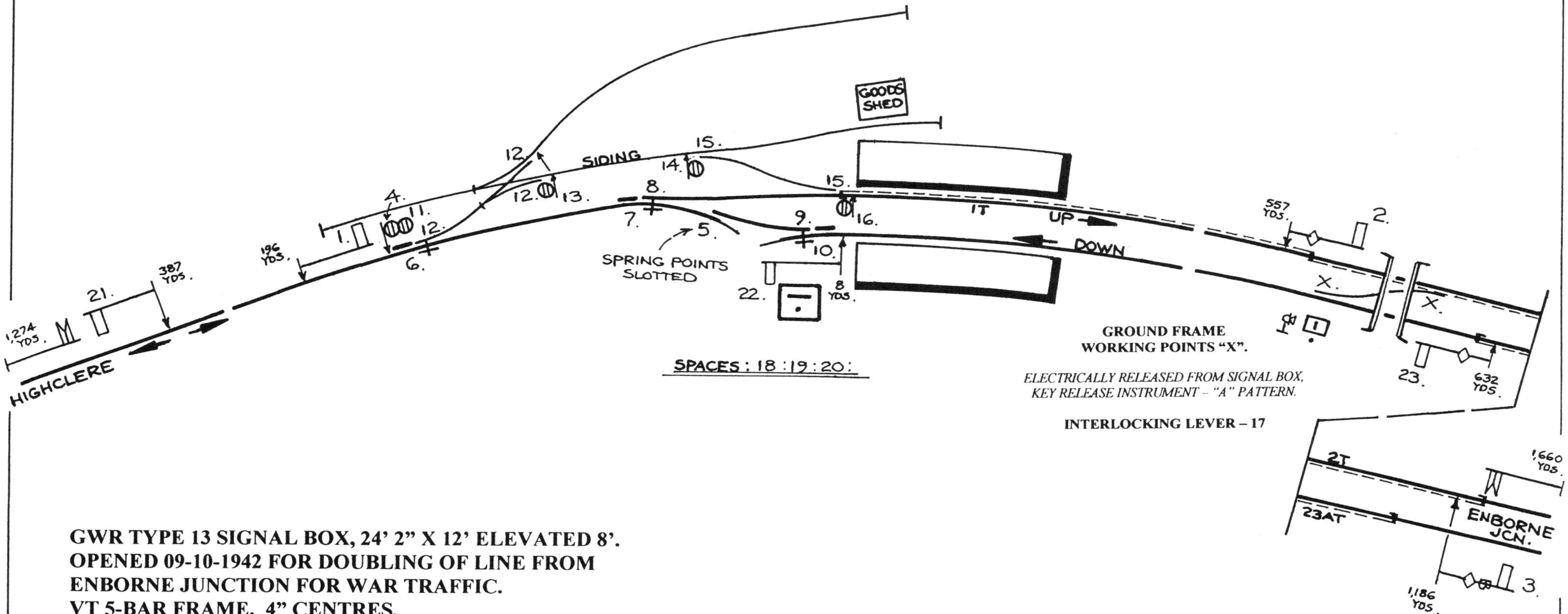

GWR TYPE 13 SIGNAL BOX, 24' 2" X 12' ELEVATED 8'.
OPENED 09-10-1942 FOR DOUBLING OF LINE FROM ENBORNE JUNCTION FOR WAR TRAFFIC.
VT 5-BAR FRAME, 4" CENTRES.
FPLs STAND NORMALLY "OUT".
ELECTRIC KEY TOKEN TO HIGHCLERE.
SPAGNOLETTI BLOCK TO ENBORNE JUNCTION.
CLOSING SWITCH:- NIL.

08-06-1964: Sidings taken out of use. Points 12, 15, FPL 6, and Discs 11, 13, 14, & 15 abolished.

BOX CLOSED 10-08-1964 (LINE CLOSED).

HERMITAGE (1943)

THIS LAYOUT OPERATIVE FROM 17-02-1943 WHEN DOUBLING OF NEWBURY – HAMPSTEAD NORRIS SECTION COMPLETED.

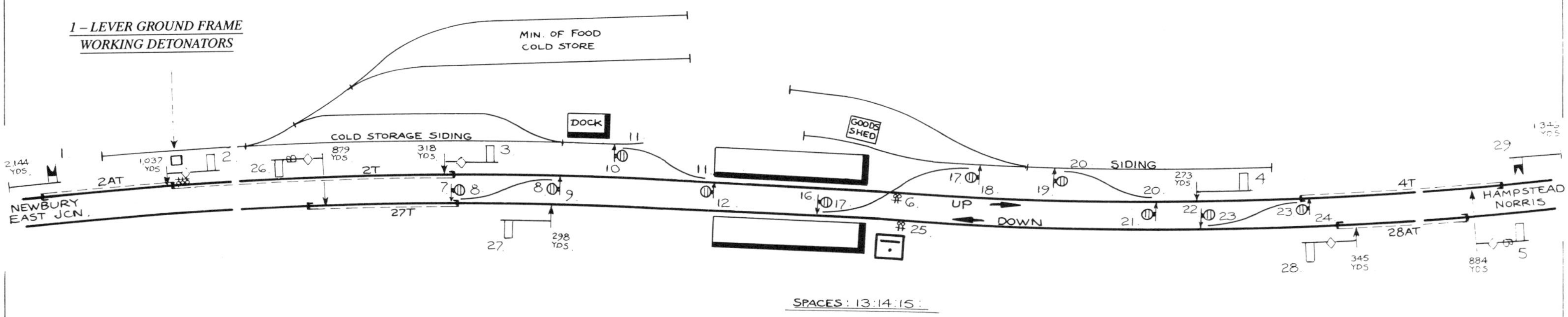

GLOS. CARRIAGE & WAGON CO. SIGNAL BOX,
OPENED 01-06-1891 WITH THAT COMPANY'S PATTERN OF LEVER FRAME. NEW 5-BAR VT FRAME, 4" CTRS, INSTALLED FOR DOUBLING WORKS 1942.
SPAGNOLETTI BLOCK (AFTER DOUBLING).
CLOSING SWITCH:- ONE (PROVIDED 1943).

BOX CLOSED 10-08-1964 (LINE CLOSED).

HAMPSTEAD NORRIS (1944)

THIS LAYOUT OPERATIVE FROM 07-03-1943 WHEN DOUBLING OF HERMITAGE – COMPTON SECTION COMPLETED.

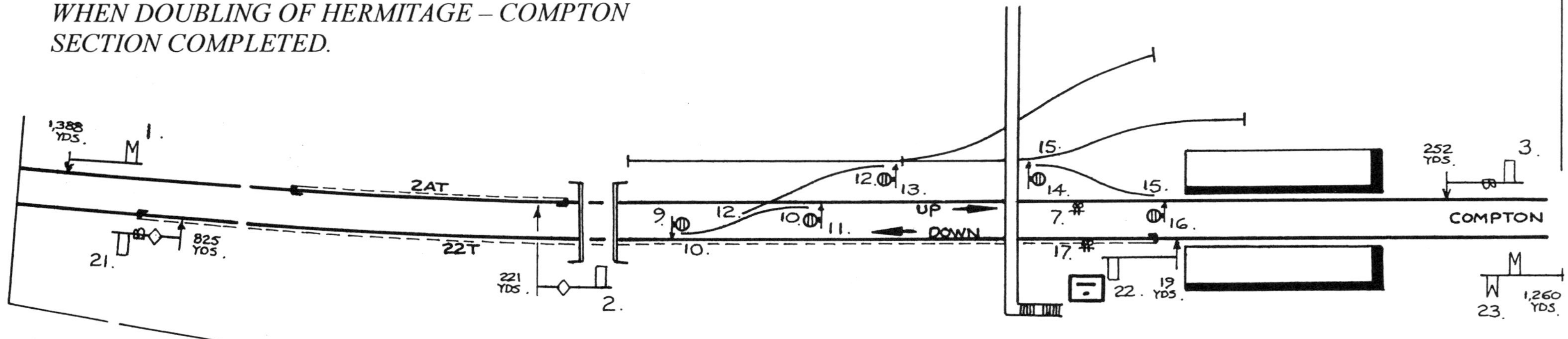

SPACES: 4:5:6:18:19:20:

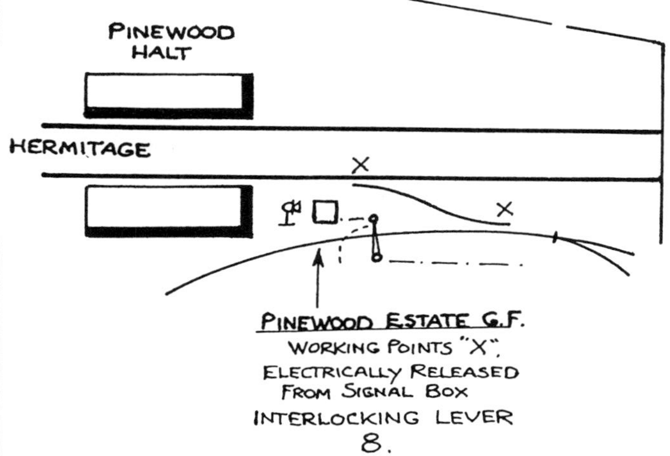

GWR TYPE 13 SIGNAL BOX, 24' 2" X 12' ELEVATED 8'.
OPENED 18-04-1943 TO REPLACE ORIGINAL R.S.C. BOX OF 1882 VINTAGE.
VT 5-BAR FRAME, 4" CENTRES.
SPAGNOLETTI BLOCK.
CLOSING SWITCH:- ONE.

BOX CLOSED 10-08-1964 (LINE CLOSED).

COMPTON (1944)

THIS LAYOUT OPERATIVE FROM 14-04-1943 WHEN DOUBLING OF HAMPSTEAD NORRIS – UPTON SECTION COMPLETED.

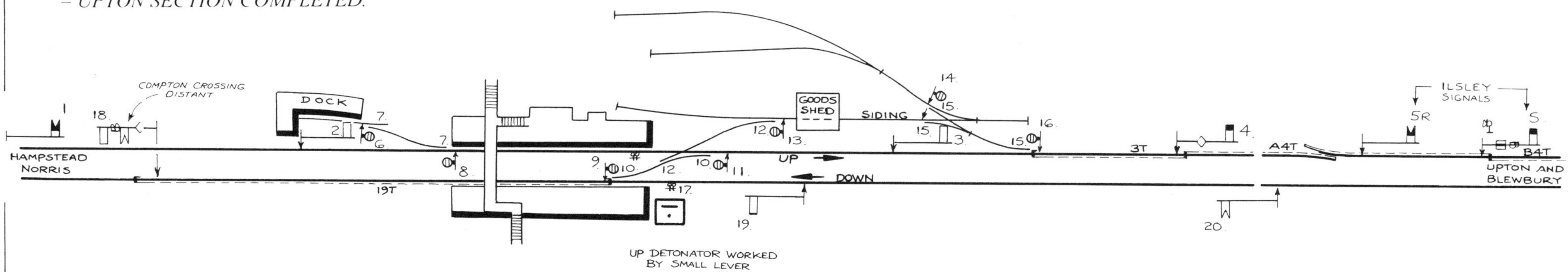

GLOS. CARRIAGE & WAGON CO. SIGNAL BOX, OPENED 1882.
ORIGINAL "GLOS" LEVER FRAME REPLACED WITH VT 3-BAR FRAME, 4" CENTRES, MARCH 1920.
SPAGNOLETTI BLOCK.
CLOSING SWITCH:- REMOVED AT DOUBLING.

BOX CLOSED 10-08-1964 (LINE CLOSED)

UPTON & BLEWBURY (1944)

THIS LAYOUT OPERATIVE FROM 14-04-1943,
WHEN DOUBLING OF LINE COMPLETED.

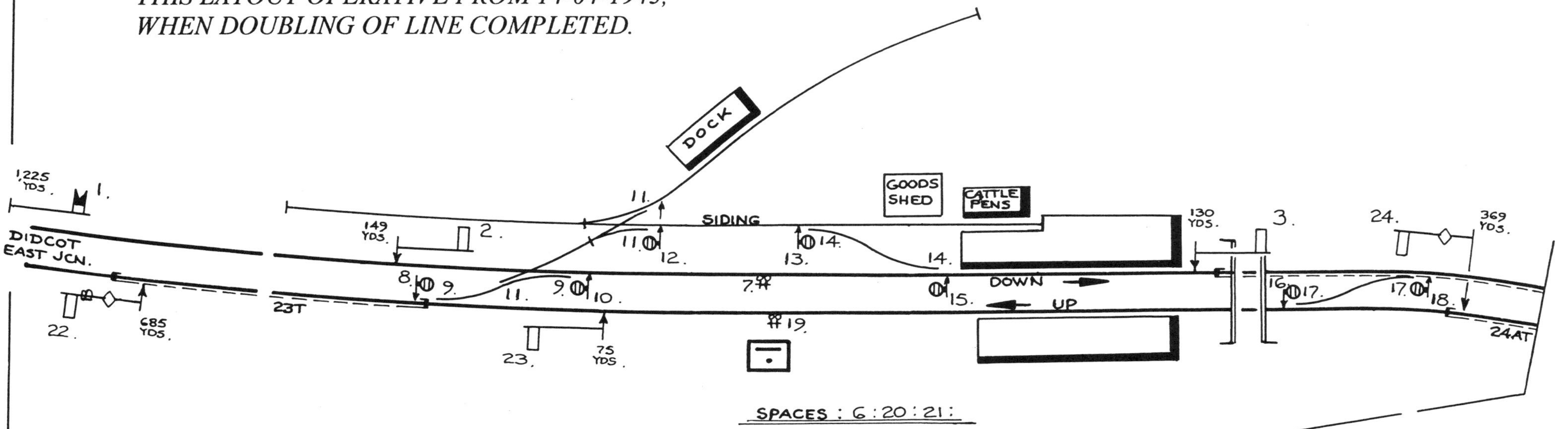

RAILWAY SIGNAL CO. BOX, OPENED 05-05-1890.
RSC FRAME REMOVED AND VT 5-BAR FRAME , 4" CENTRES, INSTALLED FEBRUARY 1943.
SPAGNOLETTI BLOCK.
CLOSING SWITCH:- ONE (ADDED AT DOUBLING).

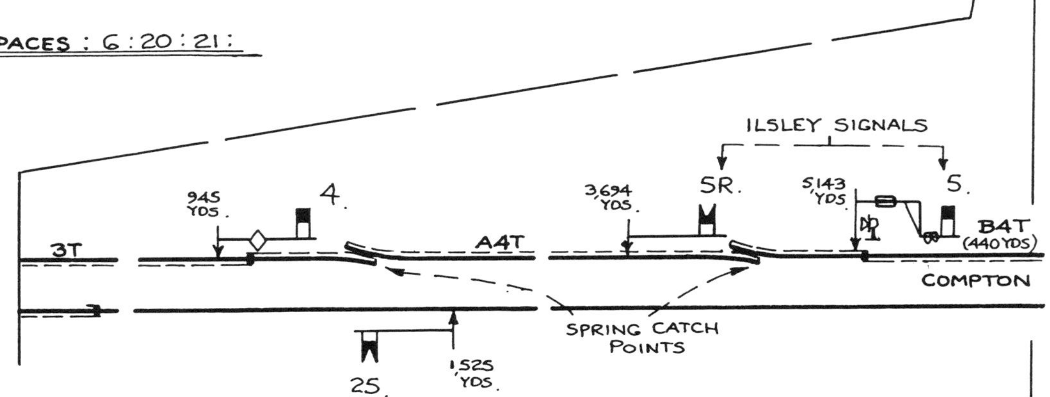

BOX CLOSED 10-08-1964 (LINE CLOSED).

SECTION FOUR

LAMBOURN BRANCH

LINE OPENED 04-04-1898.

CLOSED TO PASSENGERS AND TO ALL TRAFFIC BETWEEN WELFORD PARK AND LAMBOURN 04-01-1960.

CLOSED COMPLETELY NEWBURY TO WELFORD PARK 03-11-1973.
(FROM 19-07-1965 TRAFFIC HAD BEEN WORKED AS REQUIRED BY M.O.D.)

LAMBOURN

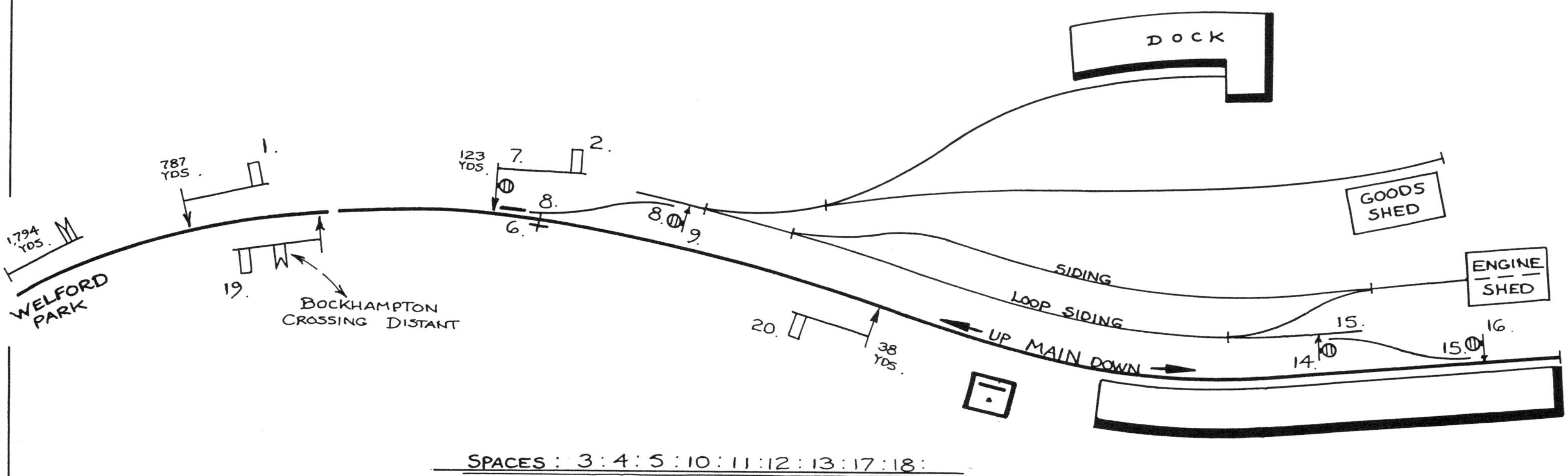

GWR TYPE 28B GROUND-LEVEL SIGNAL BOX, 17' X 10', OPENED 25-06-1910.
STUD LOCKING FRAME, 5¼" CENTRES.
FPL STANS NORMALLY "OUT".
ELECTRIC TRAIN STAFF.
CLOSING SWITCH:- NIL.

BOX CLOSED O4-01-1960 (LINE CLOSED)

WELFORD PARK (1955)

THIS LAYOUT OPERATIVE FROM 12-05-1954, WHEN AIR MINISTRY SIDINGS BROUGHT INTO USE.

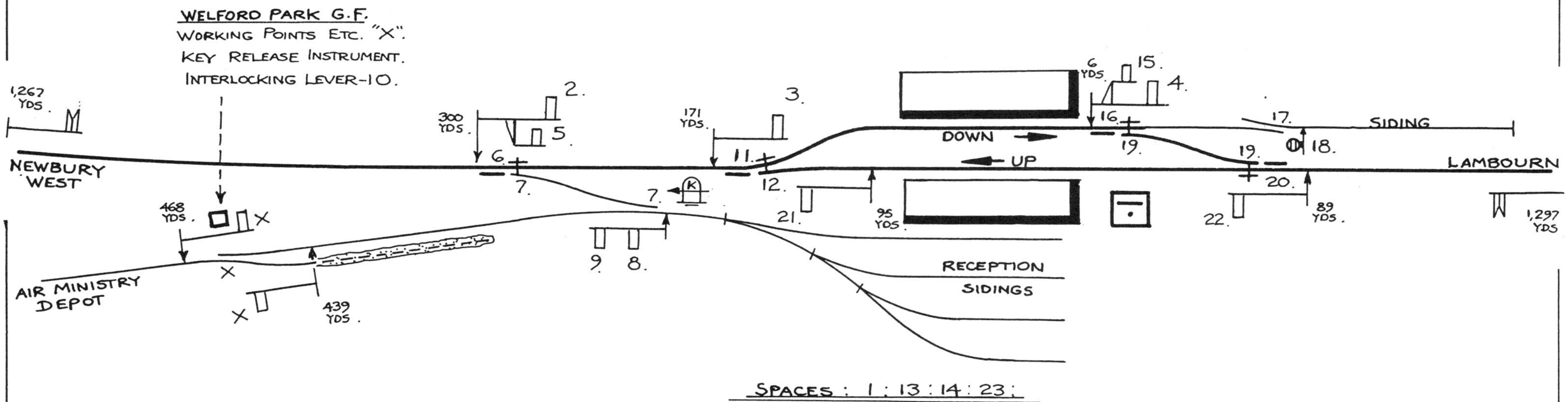

GWR TYPE 27C GROUND-LEVEL SIGNAL BOX, 21' X 11', OPENED 07-02-1909.
HT 3-BAR FRAME, 4" CENTRES, ORIGINALLY OF 16 LEVERS, CONVERTED TO TAPPET LOCKING AND EXTENDED TO 23 LEVERS SEPT. 1953.
FPLs STAND NORMALLY "OUT".
ELECTRIC TRAIN STAFF.
CLOSING SWITCH:- NIL.

04-01-1960: Line to Welford Park terminated in stop blocks 12 chains beyond 19 Points.

BOX CLOSED 03-07-1962. NEW GROUND FRAMES PROVIDED TO WORK CONNECTION TO DEPOT.

NOTES ON THE MARLBOROUGH BRANCH

No numbered diagram of Marlborough (GW) has come to light, the information shown on the diagram over being gleaned from photographs and official GWR track layout plans. The line opened on 14th April 1864. Original signalling arrangements are unclear, but in connection with the projection of Swindon, Marlborough and Andover Railway trains over the branch in 1882 a new box was opened at Marlborough South Junction and the method of working up-graded to Webb & Thompson Electric Train Staff with the branch being worked in two sections: Marlborough Station to South Junction and South Junction to Savernake West.

Marlborough Station Box was renewed in 1892 as a platform-level structure containing a 15-lever frame, but the South Junction box was abolished on 26-06-1898 when the opening of the Marlborough and Grafton Railway allowed through traffic to be diverted away from the branch. The connection between the two lines was cut on that date but was restored in 1926 for wagon exchange, the points at the GWR end being controlled by a Ground Frame.

In 1933 the GWR (who had absorbed the other lines in the area at the Grouping) embarked upon a rationalization scheme at Marlborough. Their old terminus station was closed to passengers and the central portion of the branch was removed, the Savernake-Marlborough shuttle service being diverted into the former M & SWJ station by means of a slew at Hat Gate giving access to the former Marlborough and Grafton Up Line. The latter route was also singled, giving two parallel single lines between Hat Gate and Marlborough M & SWJ station.

Marlborough terminus remained open for goods traffic via the 1926 connection, but the signal box was closed on 15-02-1933 and the points converted to hand operation. The establishment survived as "Marlborough High Level Goods" until 07-09-1964, although as freight declined the M & SW yard could usually accommodate the local traffic and the sidings were little used latterly.

MARLBOROUGH (GWR)

LAYOUT DIAGRAM ONLY – NO LEVER NUMBERS AVAILABLE (SEE NOTES).

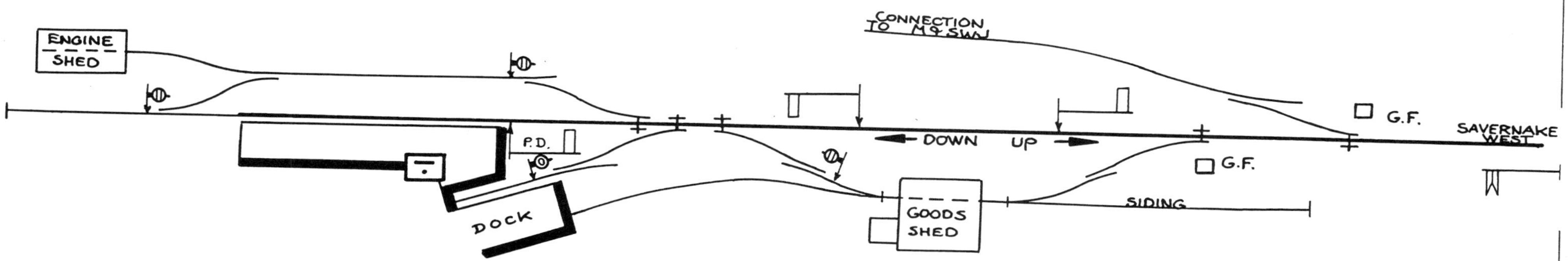